I0667434

The *50+*
Traveler's
Guidebook

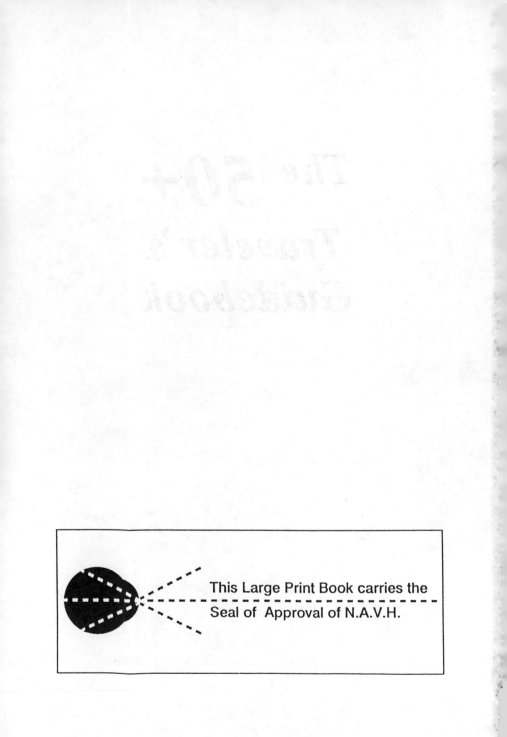

This Large Print Book carries the
Seal of Approval of N.A.V.H.

The 50+
Traveler's
Guidebook

◆ WHERE TO GO ◆
◆ WHERE TO STAY ◆
◆ WHAT TO DO ◆

Anita Williams and
Merrimac Dillon

Thorndike Press • Thorndike, Maine

Library of Congress Cataloging in Publication Data:

Williams, Anita.
   The 50+ traveler's guidebook : where to go, where to
stay, what to do / Anita Williams and Merrimac Dillon.
   p. cm.
   Includes bibliographical references and index.
   ISBN 1-56054-287-X (alk. paper : lg. print)
   ISBN 1-56054-944-0 (alk. paper : lg. print : pbk.)
   1. Aged—Travel. I. Dillon, Merrimac. II. Title.
[G151.W55   1992]   91-36809
910'.2'02—dc20   CIP

Thorndike Press Large Print edition published in 1992
by arrangement with St. Martin's Press, Inc.

Cover design by Ralph Lizotte.

The tree indicium is a trademark of Thorndike Press.

This book is printed on acid-free, high opacity paper.

*To our favorite lifelong travel companions,
Lew and Rich*

Contents

PART II

Resources

Acknowledgments

Our sincerest thanks to the Doral family, whose support made this project infinitely easier to complete.

Introduction

To present you with a leisure lifestyle book that truly fits the way you live today, it is necessary to redefine the meaning of being 50+. Until now, most of the labels have been negative and out of sync with the reality of people's lives. This book is addressed to you if:

- the notion of "senior" or "elder" is a complete turnoff;
- you find words like *sunset, autumn, September, golden,* and *silver* offensive;
- you've held the view that "senior citizens" and their clubs are for somebody else, somebody less capable, less active, less aware, and much older.

Perhaps you are into your second or third career and never plan to retire. Perhaps you have arranged your business affairs so you are semi- or completely retired already. The point is not whether or not you work. It's a matter of choice, of having options, exercising personal preference, and living life on your own terms.

You may have a physical condition that you have to work around, but you consider it an inconvenience, not a handicap.

You may have found that great relationships start (again) at 50, when the pressures of family life are lifting somewhat, when the house is empty and there are leisurely times to be shared.

Today you're more conscious than ever about your diet and exercise habits. You take scientists at their word that our real life-span potential is getting longer, so you consider "middle age" to extend right on up through retirement. You probably look considerably younger than your parents did at this age. However, as you discover signs of physical aging it's always a surprise to you, because in your mind and heart you consider yourself perpetually in your thirties or forties.

You aren't winding down but gearing up for a new career, new challenges, new adventures. You're proud of your moxie at having made it this far and you know you can handle what life sends your way.

Finally, you have the financial security to do the things you want to do and the energy to do them. You have a sense that you are freer than ever before, not settling for life but coming to see that life doesn't have to be perfect to be perfectly wonderful.

You're part of the most powerful consumer group in America today. You have choices. Lots of choices. If you're 50+ you are part of a market segment that spends 80 percent of the leisure travel dollars (*Business Week,* 3 April 1989). You control half of the discretionary income in the country and 70 percent of its assets. By the year 2025, 40 percent of the population will be 50+.

During the development of this book, careful thought was given to reflecting who you really are, so that you might actually look at the material and say "Yes, that's me!" Many readers may be surprised to find themselves lumped into a group they thought they would join at retirement. But keep in mind that even those of traditional retirement age (62 to 65) are enjoying a younger lifestyle as they continue to work and develop new interests. They generally take a younger viewpoint than did their predecessors.

Madison Avenue does not quite know how to approach you and appeal to you. When it does, it swings between several undesirable stereotyped images, none of which fits how you really live today. Advertisers may hold a particular view (displayed unattractively in laxative and denture ads) that is totally in-appropriate. And while the media struggles with it, books and newsletters aimed at telling marketers how to attract you are popping up everywhere.

Growing older is a fact of life, but for many 50+ individuals the freedom of time and money puts the accent on "growing" rather than "growing old." There are those who have the resources to come and go at will and treat themselves to leisure-time luxuries they have never enjoyed before (or, in some cases, that are an extension of the luxury they have al-ways enjoyed). For those with more time than money there are just as many extraordinary opportunities to enjoy life-expanding experi-ences, even if one eye must be on the budget.

While discounts are important to some ex-tent, it is usually the experience that counts. Generally there are budget and luxury options for just about anything you choose to do. The waters of Alaska, for example, are filled with cruise ships. There are casual, education-oriented cruises with comfortable, if modest, accommodations. Other ships wrap passengers in the cocoon of shipboard luxury to cruise up the inland waterways, offering champagne and four-star meals. The price may differ by thousands, but the breathtaking view is the same.

You may be one of the many individuals seeking broader educational experiences. You may want to take courses in subjects that are pertinent to your interests. There are organizations that provide a week or two of intensive study with a small group of inquisitive peers. You are drawn together by interest, not by tax bracket. The rates are affordable for just about anyone, yet you will find a wide variety of participants from all walks of life.

Within the ranks of RV (recreational vehicle) enthusiasts there are campers who tow economical fold-down tent-trailers and others who cruise in $150,000 land yachts. But, if this is a lifestyle you choose, you will meet at the same campgrounds and share a common love of the outdoors, regardless of your tag-along accommodations.

There is unity in diversity and a singular zest for living that can be expressed with or without a large cash outlay. However, as a group you have economic stability to live life the way that makes sense to you.

This book reflects the trends of the nineties and beyond. It takes into account who you are:

• You are likely to be still in your prime earning years.

- You are likely to have parents still alive, so it is hard to feel like the elder of the family.
- You may be quite affluent, financially independent, so that price is no object. Or at least you have enough disposable income to do what is important to you, by using shrewd budgeting.

And so for you, the 50+ consumer, here is a leisure lifestyle guide that can help you fill your life with excitement, education, and new experiences. You will find ways to stay overnight in Europe for no cost whatsoever or reserve lodging for as little as $5 or $10 at home and abroad. You also will learn about deluxe tours that may cost over $1,000 a day. You will discover how to study on shipboard or with a noted researcher in a foreign country. You will find out how to improve your health while vacationing.

An abundance of practical information makes this a convenient all-purpose reference. There's insider's information about lesser-known and remote adventures you might never find on your own. This is a lifestyle sourcebook designed to give you choices.

How to Be a Smart 50+ Travel Consumer

When compiling the information herein we were careful to select quality properties and programs that have a good reputation with the market they serve. You can expect service and accommodations consistent with the price. For example, a low-cost motor hotel can be expected to be clean and pleasant, but frill-free. And knowing that "roughing it" to some is a backpack trip and to others a motel in a small community, we have tried throughout to give you clues to the lifestyle enjoyed in particular places. The grand old hotels tend to be more affluent, as an example. Some cruises are all ball gowns and tuxedos, but others are denim.

We have presented those leisure-time suppliers that have had a consistently good reputation. Although we have not rated these, you will recognize many as recipients of top awards year after year. We also strongly suggest that you listen to your friends and consult a travel agent, who often will have insights into particular adventures that may be of interest to you. One person's dream vacation is another's horror story, so *ask*. You can call many places toll-free to make personal inquiries, too.

Learn to listen for "travel-speak," which fills brochures with tempting phrases. Your "romantic, isolated beach" may simply mean you are so far from civilization that no one can get there. "Quaint" may mean old, not charming. A promise of "fun, fun, fun" may be of the social director rah-rah variety, which is fine, provided that that is what you are looking for in a vacation. Go ahead — be skeptical. Better to spend time investigating and preplanning than to be disappointed.

Certain price ranges have been indicated in this book, simply to give you an idea of the economic bracket. Then you can request further information with more intelligence. Remember, prices change rapidly in the travel industry, and they are subject to increase without notice. It's prudent to double-check all pricing information or discount opportunities. More likely, with the growing awareness of the consumer power of the 50+ group, discounts will be expanded rather than lessened or eliminated. Be prepared for some pleasant surprises.

◆ PART I ◆

Where to Go, Where to Stay, What to Do: Places That Cater to Your Lifestyle

Do Something, Learn Something Vacations

Live and Learn: Travel and Educational Opportunities

There's a new trend that blends interesting subjects and wonderful vacation destinations. Sometimes called "soft learning," these courses, classes, seminars, expeditions, and excursions are the vacations of substance chosen by many adults. These learning vacations may take place on a ship, at a mountain hotel, at a luxury hotel, or on a campus here or abroad.

You may not have time for a semester in finance, but a hotel-sponsored weekend conducted by financial experts may tell you all you need to know. You may have a problem breaking free for a lecture series on ecology, but you may find a few days to join a wildlife expedition or bird count.

In fact, many of the courses offered at lodges, at resorts, on cruise ships, or in other relaxing environments may not be available anywhere else! Many people who cannot justify a "vacation" can reserve a few days for a seminar without any twinge of guilt.

And the exciting twist is that you always get to meet new people who share your interests and enthusiasm. Many annual events draw repeat guests year after year to renew old friendships and to learn something new.

Hotel Programs

The Cloister
100 First Street
Sea Island, GA 31561
(912) 638-3611
800-SEA-ISLAND

This resort sponsors so many courses that there's room to list only a sampling here. Suffice it to say that guests love these opportunities to learn while enjoying the traditional elegance of the resort. Many return year after year for their favorite events.

- The annual bridge festivals are a winter tradition full of pageantry and great fun. All levels of players can find suitable partners.
- Big bands provide music for nostalgic dances and romantic weekends.

- A Wildlife Weekend provides a minisafari with scholarly researchers to explore and photograph wildlife. Choose to track sea life, birds, or animals. Expeditions are educational and the proceeds from a lively auction benefit the Georgia Nongame Wildlife Fund.
- A Financial Planning Seminar brings in experts to teach you how to make the most of your resources.
- The Cloister Food and Wine Classic provides several days of expert instruction on wine selection and haute cuisine.
- The Cloister Garden Series is an annual program developed to help you design your home's landscape with a professional touch. Renowned horticulturists and garden editors participate in the program.

Contact the resort for a complete listing of the year's events. Prepare to meet interesting and involved individuals who share your passion for life.

The Greenbrier
Station A
White Sulphur Springs, WV 24986
(304) 536-1110
800-624-6070
 The Greenbrier, one of this country's grand

traditional hotels, has become famous for its cooking schools. Spend a week enjoying the resort and improving your culinary skills. You'll learn how to use the newest kitchen equipment as well as classic utensils to prepare exciting menus. Each day's classes cover a different style of cuisine. You and classmates will be treated to a champagne reception and a Greenbrier Gold Service Dinner (the ultimate!).

Expect to pay more than $1,200 at this deluxe hotel for your five-day stay. The cost includes a double-occupancy room, two meals daily, course tuition, and many extras. This qualifies as an affluent adventure, yet it is one that will give you solid cooking skills and a sociable week at a posh resort.

Leen's Lodge
Box 40
Grand Lake Stream, ME 04637
(207) 947-7284 (winter)
(207) 796-5575 (summer)
L. L. Bean information: 800-341-4341, ext. 3100

Every year L. L. Bean holds an exclusive fly fishing school during the summer at this wilderness retreat. Two sessions can accommodate just 12 students each, with expert instructors giving personal attention to each participant. Each school session is slightly different, but in the past they have been four-day, three-night events costing in the neighborhood of $1,000 for tuition, lodging, and meals. You must plan to reserve well in advance for these classes, as their popularity and limited enrollment makes space a premium!

See also the listing for Rivermeadows in "The Ranch Experience," later in this chapter. They sponsor fly fishing schools as well; contact them for details.

Mohonk Mountain House
New Paltz, NY 12561
(914) 255-1000

There's always something going on at Mohonk. If it's not a family reunion it's Cooking Weekend. Or perhaps a mind-stretching Word Weekend or a total-immersion Foreign Language Weekend better suits your style. A variety of workshops and special programs fill the calendar year-round at the Mohonk. And, of course, these are the folks who brought the Mystery Weekend into vogue. A mystery play is enacted and you get to help solve the crime. And what a perfect nook-and-cranny mansion for it, too!

Check with the hotel for the complete schedule and choose what looks interesting to you. It all seems like too much fun to be "educational," but you'll always learn something at a Mohonk event.

The Mystery Weekend costs about $1,000 for two persons and includes three meals a day, the program, and taxes. Other programs use their normal tariff schedule, which allows two people to stay for anywhere from about $160 per night (room, basin only) up to $250 for the higher-priced regular guest rooms. Prices include three meals daily.

Palm Beach Polo and Country Club
13198 Forest Hill Boulevard
West Palm Beach, FL 33414
(407) 798-7000
800-327-4204
Fax: 407-798-7052

If you have ever wanted to learn to play the sport of kings, take advantage of this unusual school. Every February through April the club offers Major Hugh Dawnay's Polo Vision Clinics.

These week-long courses cost $1,250 at this writing (expect annual increases) and include 28 hours of instruction, polo ponies to ride, a complimentary copy of Dawnay's *Polo Vision* book, attendance at an international match, plus social events. The clinics are supplemented by personal coaching.

In addition to the courses available at hotels and resorts, several programs have been developed that provide exciting educational experiences and, in some cases, combine your educational experience with low-cost accommodations.

Travel-Study

American Youth Hostels
Box 37613
Washington, D.C. 20013-7613
(202) 783-6161

Don't think economical travel is the divine right of youth. American Youth Hostels (AYH) has expanded its programs to meet the demands of the budget-wise 50+ traveler. AYH is known for its backpacking and cycling tours, but there are motor trips as well. All programs are open to anyone fit enough to keep up with the group. There are also some tours specifically of interest for the 50+ group. Expect to learn about history and more as you travel.

Your AYH card will give you entrance to approximately 5,000 hostels worldwide through sister organizations in 69 other countries. You typically will find dormitory-style lodgings that cost $5 to $13 per night. A reduced membership fee of $15 is offered to those over 55.

Each property is different; some are spartan, some quaint. Knowing that this is the budget route for travel, you may want to hand-pick your properties using the *AYH Handbook*. Be aware that some hostels expect you to arrive on foot, bicycle, or public transportation, in keeping with their purpose. This is not the option for you if you expect to be waited on; everyone pitches in to help at a hostel.

Anderson Ranch Arts Center
Box 5598
Snowmass Village, CO 81615
(303) 923-3181

A nonprofit arts organization, the ranch offers about eighty one- or two-week summer courses in ceramics, photography, woodworking, painting, sculpture, and mixed media. There is also a children's program. You will stay in a dorm with either a private or a shared bath. Your food and lodging will run less than $50 per day. Tuition costs range from $250 to $450, depending on the class. Because the ranch is close to Aspen, you will find plenty of recreational and cultural diversions.

Audubon Ecology Camps and Workshops
National Audubon Society
613 Riversville Road
Greenwich, CT 06831
(203) 869-2017

Learn to photograph landscapes, wild-flowers, insects, and wild game from professional photographers. The ten-day trip will put you in three different locations for a variety of photo opportunities. Accommodations are rustic log cabins. The price is less than $100 per day and includes lodging, tuition, and most meals.

Canyonlands Field Institute
Box 68
Moab, UT 84532
(801) 259-7750

This nonprofit organization offers a variety of programs, from one-day seminars to five-day tours, so you can study ecology, archaeology, natural history, and cultural history. Day trips are reasonably priced, from under $50 per day. The tours, which include lodging, run about $100 per day.

Close-Up Foundation
44 Canal Center Plaza
Arlington, VA 22314
(703) 892-5428
800-232-2000

Get an insider's view of Washington, D.C., with this program developed in cooperation with the American Association of Retired Persons (AARP). You'll get behind closed doors and speak with elected officials and their staff to discuss current events that influence your life. You will gain new insight into the democratic process. During the week-long session, you will meet other involved adults from around the country. The program is comfortably paced and professionally guided every step of the way.

Because the foundation is specifically designed to serve older Americans and get them more actively involved in government issues, the prices are deliberately kept reasonable. A week-long trip will cost you about $100 a day, which includes six or seven nights' accommodations, all meals, ground transportation, baggage handling, gratuities and taxes, instructors, tours, seminars, and sightseeing. Plus they will give you the Close-Up publication and arrange for theater tickets and sightseeing for after-hours. A rare bonus: an insurance policy for life, health, and accident during your trip. You can tell that the AARP has had a hand in planning this!

Be sure to ask about their auxiliary trips, such as the intergenerational weeks or the two-city trips, which combine Washington, D.C., and either Williamsburg or Philadelphia.

Earthwatch
Box 403N
680 Mount Auburn Street
Watertown, MA 02172
(617) 926-8200

Here is a way to make a difference in life. Join an expedition and become a volunteer to a renowned researcher. Choose a subject that interests you, from archaeology to zoology, and travel to one of the 85 countries where research sites are located. More than half of the research sites are in the U.S. and almost half of the volunteers are over 46 years old.

You may stay in a tent, a castle, or a university dormitory. You will live and work with a team to support projects that aid the environment or help endangered wildlife. Some research experiences are more strenuous, so inquire carefully. Within a given research compound, jobs range from low activity (watching baby monkeys nurse) to high activity (tracking older monkeys up a hillside). Whatever your interests or level of physical fitness, you should be able to be matched with a program that will help you learn something new and let you participate in an adventure that can influence the future of the planet.

Your tax-deductible contribution will cover your living expenses and help support the efforts of the research team. Costs vary with each program, from $700 to as much as $5,000, with the average being about $1,200 to $1,300 for two weeks. You must arrange your own transportation, but once there, your food and lodging are covered. Participants must belong to Earthwatch (membership is $25), but information also will be sent to interested inquirers.

Elderhostel
75 Federal St.
Boston, MA 02109
(617) 426-7788

This may be one of the great educational travel bargains available. Elderhostel, a non-profit organization, has a program designed especially for the inquisitive 60+ traveler. With a network of more than twelve hundred universities worldwide, Elderhostel can provide low-cost accommodations while offering stimulating lecture programs. You will stay in the dormitory, eat in the cafeteria, take courses from the resident professors, and enjoy field trips through the area. A few specialty programs are offered at nonacademic sites, but all provide quality educational opportunities. Study architecture, ecology, photography, computers, the fine arts. It would be difficult not to find something of interest in their catalog.

The typical domestic program lasts one week, costs about $250, and includes six nights' accommodations, all meals, five days of classes, and many extracurricular activities. International experiences last two weeks or more with comparable tuition costs, but since the cost includes airfare, prices vary dramatically, depending on your destination.

This is not a glamorous experience, but it is a fulfilling one. Dorms are not the accommodation of choice for many and cafeteria food not everyone's favorite. However, this is an ideal way to take a vacation with interesting people, even if your budget is pinched. Don't make the mistake of thinking this option is only for penny-pinchers, however. Many affluent people seek out these courses, even when they can afford luxurious accommodations, because it is a great opportunity to meet many other active, intelligent people and experience new cultures in depth.

The enthusiastic response of the participants has drawn an ever-increasing enrollment.

Nearly 200,000 individuals enjoy the programs every year.

Interhostel
University of New Hampshire
6 Garrison Avenue
Durham, NH 03824
(603) 862-1147
800-SEE-WRLD

In cooperation with sister institutions in other countries, the University of New Hampshire can open a new world of travel and education to the 50+ traveler. The purpose of the program, part of the university's continuing education department, is to promote cross-cultural understanding and to give participants the chance to experience another country at a deeper level.

Every trip includes courses taught by the professors of your host institution, the lowest applicable airfares, all meals and accommodations, access to local activities and attractions, and much more. The all-inclusive price averages about $100 per day. You will be part of a small group, which is ideal for learning and sharing. You will stay in university housing or modest hotels nearby. The trips are generally two weeks in length and attract a lively, intelligent group of people from many walks of life.

International Friendship Service
22994 El Toro Road
El Toro, CA 92630
(714) 458-8868

This private cultural organization offers an overseas study program. You can learn a language or improve your French, Italian, or Spanish. If you pass the final, you'll receive a diploma stating that you passed the course. Usually you will stay on campus; however, some students stay with families that live within walking distance of the university. By staying several weeks in your chosen city you will have the opportunity to absorb the local culture.

Trips last three to four weeks. Prices vary with each school, the length of stay, and on whether airfare is included. However, as a guide, trips (before airfare) can range from about $600 for a two-week stay to about $2,000 for a month-long trip, meals, lodging, and tuition included. You must read their program guide to appreciate the variety of options open to you.

You may participate in a slightly different way by hosting foreign students for one, two, or three weeks during the summer. As with most programs of this kind, the number of applicants always seems to outstrip the availability of host homes.

National Registration Center for Study Abroad
823 North 2nd Street
Milwaukee, WI 53202
(414) 278-0631
800-558-9988

This organization represents eighty-five schools abroad that offer subject or language courses. Students stay in pensions (bed and breakfast-style accommodations) or private homes. Costs are as low as $235 per week including accommodations in a host home, tuition, and more. Send a self-addressed stamped envelope (45¢ postage required) for information.

Mexico Study Groups
Box 56982
Phoenix, AZ 85079
(602) 242-9231

To experience Mexico in depth, you may enjoy two weeks or a month with this experienced travel-study group. You can study the language, learn about the history and culture of the country, or take art classes. Depending on the program you choose, you might stay in a hotel or with local families. This is also an ideal orientation for you if the idea of relocating to Mexico is appealing. Trips may take you to Mérida, capital of Yucatán state, Cuernavaca, or the small colonial town of San Miguel de Allende.

Your trip will include accommodations, tuition, and some excursions. Prices range from around $800 for two weeks to around $1,000 for a month. Each travel-study program is unique and has its own features, so these prices are given only as a guideline, to give you some sense of the price range. Annual increases should be expected.

Sierra Club
730 Polk Street
San Francisco, CA 94109
(415) 776-2211

National and international trips to help the environment can be taken with the Sierra Club (where and when change constantly). You also can participate in local programs organized by the group in your area. Contact the main office for current information and for a referral to the group nearest you. The modestly priced programs vary in length and price.

Skidmore College
North Broadway
Saratoga Springs, NY 12866
(518) 584-5000

Study the medieval and renaissance eras in Florence, Italy, with experts on a two-week study-vacation offered by Skidmore College.

You will visit museums, cathedrals, gardens, and other locales, where on-site teaching will bring art and history to life for you and your companions. You will stay in a comfortable pension with a private bath in your room. Free time for shopping and personal exploration is planned into your schedule.

Expect the cost to run $2,500 or more, which includes round-trip airfare from New York to Rome, ground transportation, tuition, housing, two meals daily, and some excursions. Prices will fluctuate annually according to airfare costs.

Sotheby's Educational Studies
1334 York Avenue
New York, NY 10021
(212) 606-7822
Fax: 212-606-7949

If fine art and antiques fascinate you, contact Sotheby's to find out about their lecture series, one-day seminars, connoisseurship seminars, and travel seminars. Prices range from about $125 for one-day seminars to about $1,000 for the four-day travel seminar. These are taught by distinguished scholars and renowned professionals using exquisite public and private collections as the examples for your class. Most courses are conducted in New York, but Los Angeles is another seminar site;

the travel seminars to explore regional art are a good option for out-of-towners.

Sotheby's Educational Studies
30 Oxford Street
London, England WIR 1RE
Phone: 9 011 44 71 408 1100
Fax: 9 011 44 71 408 8160

For an antique buff, what could be more enticing than an "insiders" course in Scotland or England. You must contact the London office directly for this adventure.

WANT EVEN MORE OPTIONS?

Also see the AARP listing in the "Clubs and Association" chapter. They have travel/study programs available to members. Refer also to the section on cruises (page 207), where you will find a number of floating classrooms, ranging from Alaskan shipboard seminars to lectures offered by Cunard, Princess, Pearl Cruises, and others, to the computer room aboard the QE2 to sharpen your skills.

Check with colleges in your area if you wish to audit a course. When you audit, you don't take tests or receive credit. As a 50+ "visitor," frequently you pay little or nothing for the privilege of sitting in on classes. State schools seem to be more open to this concept; in fact, some states mandate that citizens of a certain age have access to the classroom.

Wilderness Programs

American Wilderness Adventures
Box 1486
Boulder, CO 80306
(303) 494-2992
800-444-0099

These are the same fun folks who plan the Guest Ranch Vacations (see "The Ranch Experience"). They can send you packing on horseback trips or rushing down the rapids on a white water raft. You can trek with the llamas or sail in Hawaii. Every page of their adventure catalog is a temptation.

American Wilderness Adventures bills itself as "the civilized way to rough it," so that gives you a clue as to the somewhat "controlled" nature of the adventure. Each trip is different, ranging from tent or cabin accommodations to a deluxe comfort-conscious Alaskan safari. For backcountry trips they ask that you be physically fit or, as they aptly state, "old enough to get on a horse and young enough to stay on." Take that as your clue to investigate each adventure to see if it suits your fitness level and desire for comfort.

These people are excited to have 50+ folks

along and even have a company policy that should be industry-wide; they will get on the phone with you and tell you exactly what you need to know about the trip. If you have any special physical or dietary restrictions, they can help you choose a trip that is appropriate for you. And there are discounts available on many of the trips, so be sure to ask!

Their prices range from less than $100 a day for short "Laid Back Trips" by canoe to about $150 per day for week-long trips to Hawaii or Mexico. A handful are more costly, but they are the exception. Prices include just about everything: accommodations, hearty meals, equipment, and instructions. You'll need to bring your personal things and a warm sleeping bag. You won't have to guess; they will provide a list of clothing and essentials.

If you have longed for a wilderness experience but don't have the courage or expertise to plan one on your own, this program is certainly a good option. However, don't forget that even when well planned by experienced pros, wilderness trips have inherent risks. The company recommends a medical exam before your trip and will require you to sign a release.

Outdoor Vacations for Women Over 40
Box 200
Groton, MA 01450
(508) 448-3331

Choose your challenge: a day trip, a weekend excursion, or week-long vacation. Every season brings a new set of adventures for 40+ women. You may choose a hiking weekend in the Berkshires or to explore the forests of Costa Rica. Program founder Marion Stoddart is an internationally known conservationist.

Participants have varying degrees of abilities, so don't be intimidated by the prospect of trying something new. You will stay in country inns, in rustic lodges, or, when rafting, under the stars in a sleeping bag. Best of all, you can share your adventure with mature women who want to experience life in a new way.

The program includes several intriguing day trips, such as the Wild Edible Workshop, that run about $50 per day. The longer excursions, such as the Galápagos trip, which shuttles you by yacht from island to island, cost approximately $2,600. The price includes meals, lodging, transfers, equipment, instruction, and gratuities.

The program changes every year, as do the prices, so if interested, check on current programs and costs.

Outward Bound
384 Field Point Road
Greenwich, CT 06830
(203) 661-0797
800-243-8520

At some time in our lives, we each want to discover what we are made of, what we are capable of achieving, what challenges we can face and overcome. Outward Bound will help you make these self-discoveries. The oldest and largest of the adventure-based educational organizations in this country, Outward Bound operates five schools in Colorado, Maine, Minnesota, North Carolina, and Oregon.

Small groups of 8–12 people are guided through wilderness courses that are meant to stretch your abilities. Every effort is made to keep participants within safe and structured guidelines. You will develop specific skills for the activity at hand plus more generalized teamwork and leadership skills. Participants frequently report gaining enormous self-confidence as they meet the challenges put before them.

Choose the adventure you want: back-packing, canyoneering, dogsledding, winter camping, sailing, or white water rafting, to name a few. Many of the courses are pretty tough, so you will want to choose carefully.

It may be more appropriate to select one of the specialized courses: a three-day or four-day course for women's empowerment, another for couples, or one just for cancer patients and their families. There are also special courses for those 55 and older (the nine-day Going Beyond course), although participants can choose any course that is interesting. Costs vary from program to program. Most are moderately priced from $80 to $110 per day.

The joy of Outward Bound is discovering new depth in yourself. The experience will help you redefine and expand your limits so that life takes on a new perspective.

Your instructor will be deeply experienced in your chosen activity. All instructors are Red Cross and CPR trained; 40 percent are emergency medical technicians. Their ages range from 22 to 66.

If you are at a turning point in your life, or if your world has been closing in on you, an Outward Bound experience may be just the adventure you need to help you move confidently into a new phase of your life.

Outward Bound provides a nonsmoking, nondrinking environment.

Hunting and Fishing

If you've been waiting all your life for the ultimate hunting or fishing trip, there are some experiences awaiting you that may end up being the highlight of your life. These hand-picked sport paradises offer some adventures that many have enjoyed. Catering to men and women who have the means and the time to seek out the best, these may be among a handful of places where you can enjoy a true wilderness experience. A trip may cost several thousand dollars for a week-long adventure.

Alaska Sports Fishing Lodge Association
500 Wall Street, Suite 422
Seattle, WA 98121
(206) 448-4477
800-352-2003

Contact this association for up-to-date information about fishing in Alaska. The group was formed by a number of reputable lodges to help fishers find the ideal place to suit their Alaskan fishing dream.

With guidance from this organization, you can determine where in the vast Alaskan wilderness to find "your" spot in your price range. You may arrange a short stay of a few days or a week. In general, these are not inexpensive trips, but this organization can direct you to the least expensive, or most expensive, places.

Falcon
PO Box 1899
Bangor, ME 04402-1899
(207) 990-4534
800-825-8234

As one guest describes it, "it's like living a National Geographic special." Falcon operates two magnificent locations, one in western Maine and the other in northern Maine.

To get to either locale, a Falcon guide will meet you at the Bangor International Airport and take you to the departure base, where a float plane will fly you into the Maine wilderness. That trip alone will introduce you to the natural beauty and wildlife seldom seen by humans.

If you choose the luxurious Spencer Lake camp you'll be in the mountainous region of the state. Every personal touch lets you know you're roughing it in style. Spencer Lake provides a four-star chef to create your gourmet meals and top-of-the-line sporting gear to insure your pleasure. The more modest Musquacook Lodge in northern Maine provides a less formal, less expensive outdoor experience.

If you want a truly backwoods experience, Falcon also provides the Drop Camp. Specially selected locations have been found on some of Maine's least accessible lakes, where camps, complete with fully equipped wall tents, make your stay comfortable.

For hunters there are 40,000 acres of privately controlled land, giving you an excellent chance for a trophy. Maine black bears frequently exceed 200 pounds. Moose and deer roam freely. There's also excellent partridge and woodcock hunting and year-round hunting of coyotes.

For fishers, there are guides who know the waters. You'll be flown by float plane to inaccessible ponds and creeks. Fly-fish, spin fish, or troll for your catch. For nature lovers there's white water rafting and unparalleled beauty.

The one-price-covers-all policy lets you choose the level that suits your style and budget, but in general expect a high price tag to match the elite nature of the experience.

You can learn about Falcon by watching an enticing video; a $15 deposit (credited against any future stay) will bring 18 minutes of unforgettable video to your VCR. You will see why this lodge commands top dollar.

King Salmon Lodge
Providence Professional Building
3300 Providence Drive, Suite 309
Anchorage, AK 99508
(907) 562-2275 (day)
(907) 277-3033 (evening)

If you're an accomplished fisher and haven't heard about Mike Cusak's King Salmon Lodge, it's time you discovered this amazing Alaskan retreat. Major sports magazines and outdoor TV programs rave about the adventures available at this lodge.

At several thousand dollars per week per person, this is a first-class operation. However, guests wanting the very best in a fishing holiday will not be disappointed. The video showing anglers excitedly reeling in trophy catches has such you-are-there realism, you will want to grab your gear and head out that minute.

Mike's place is completely surrounded by trophy-filled waters. But to give you an even better chance at landing the fish of your dreams, seaplanes fly you to secret fishing spots where Mike has left boats to reach otherwise inaccessible wilderness locations.

Fish with fly or lure from June through October. Most fish — rainbow trout, arctic char, Dolly Varden, arctic grayling, lake trout, Northern pike, and king calico salmon

— are available much of the season. August brings the salmon for fantastic fishing in late summer and early fall. The lodge ardently supports the catch-and-release program, which allows you to keep your legal limit but return other fish caught.

The fishing is only one element of the adventure. With the wildlife abundant in the area, seaplane tours and day-long float trips for photographers and nature lovers are popular as well.

The food is hearty and plentiful. The accommodations resemble what you'd expect a wealthy relative's "rustic" lodge to look like. You have all that woodsy ambience without sacrificing comfort or style. There is a reason why this is considered the "ultimate."

Leen's Lodge
Box 40
Grand Lake Stream, ME 04637
(207) 947-7284 (winter)
(207) 796-5575

Groups of up to 20 can enjoy the "Lean-to" accommodations at Leen's Lodge. Couples or small groups can choose rustic cabins or a room in the motel unit. Whatever accommodations you choose, it will have all the cabin-in-the-woods feeling without any of the discomfort of primitive living. However, if you're a confirmed hotel dweller used to lots of fancy service, stay in the city. Life here is for the country-hearted.

This is an idyllic escape for fishermen and bird hunters, but anyone who appreciates nature will find the lodge a welcome wilderness retreat. With landlocked salmon, smallmouth bass, togue or lake trout, brook trout, white perch, and pickerel, you can find the kind of fishing adventure you may have thought no longer existed.

The guides who live in the area, paid on a per-day basis, are amply experienced to reveal the secrets of the surrounding lakes and streams. You will get to enjoy gliding through the waters in one of the Grand Laker hand-built cedar canoes that are made in the town of Grand Lake Stream.

Fly fishermen are particularly fond of the many excellent fishing adventures in the area. For several years L. L. Bean has held an Advanced Fly Fishing School at the lodge. A lucky dozen fishermen get to learn from experts in each of the two sessions.

Meals at the lodge include hearty Maine fare. You might take lunch on the shore, enjoying a picnic, packed by the chef, complemented by pan-fried fish — your morning's catch. Dinner is served with sunset views from the dining room.

Prices range from about $65 to $80 per person, per night. Breakfast and dinner are included. This is one of those wonderful hideaways you can't wait to discover — and hope no one else does!

If you have a physical disability, refer to the chapter on "The Handicapped Traveler" for information about the magazine *Disabled Outdoors*, which features information on access to hunting and fishing as well as other sports, plus product information to make sports easier and more enjoyable.

The Ranch Experience

When the rush of daily life threatens to smother you and the thought of a typical resort just isn't very exciting, think about taking a few days, or even a couple of weeks, in ranch country. With horseback riding, expansive skies, cookouts, real-life wranglers, and a laid-back schedule in sync with nature, a ranch may be just the alternative you need.

Many ranches today offer far more than horseback riding. Often there are surprising amenities; at the Home Ranch, for example, you can have your own heated Jacuzzi on the front porch of your rustic cabin. Most ranches have both winter and summer programs.

The ranches selected for your consideration have a wonderful mix of family-oriented activities (when you want to include the grandchildren) and all-adult activities (when you want to escape with your mate or friends). They already have demonstrated an appeal to, and consideration of, the adventurous 50+ guest.

Absaroka Ranch
Star Route
Dubois, WY 82513
(307) 455-2275

This secluded hideaway offers plenty of activity yet the kind of solitude that puts you in touch with nature and yourself. Sitting at the headwaters of Wyoming's Wind River in the shadow of the Absaroka mountain range, this ranch has a family-style approach that encourages you to meet other guests and develop new friendships.

Enjoy horseback riding on miles of high country trails or take a fishing excursion. Explore the territory on foot or let the experienced guides show you the wonder of the Tetons or Wind River.

You can relax around the campfire and sleep in rustic cabins. Meals are hearty, as you'd expect, and served family-style. Drop your pretensions and let a generations-old life-style give you a new perspective.

The cost is about $100 per day, which includes lodging, food, and full use of the facilities and horses.

Jet service is available to Jackson Hole, Wyoming. Transportation to the ranch is available for a nominal fee.

C Lazy U Ranch
PO Box 378
Granby, CO 80446
(303) 887-3344

For a ranch vacation whose emphasis is on horseback riding, this Colorado property has it all, including the same high ratings you look for in city hotels. Family-oriented, you can take along your grandchildren, who will have fun participating in special supervised programs. Or opt for the adults-only weeks in January, February, and September.

You will be assigned your own horse for your entire stay. The rides through the different terrains are guided by expert wranglers. In winter trade the saddle for skis and take off cross-country.

Back at the ranch you will enjoy family-style meals. There's also tennis, swimming, racquetball, fishing, and more.

It is most convenient to drive, but you can

fly to Denver and rent a car to drive the 97 miles to the ranch. A week's summer stay, which is more economical than by the night, is about $1,200. Day rates are upward of $200 per night, per person. Prices include meals and all ranch activities. Note: this ranch does not accept credit cards.

The Home Ranch
PO Box 822
Clark, CO 80428
(303) 879-1780 (in Colorado)
800-223-7094

The *Los Angeles Times* describes The Home Ranch as "a peaceful chuck-it-all wilderness retreat." It has won some of the most prestigious awards available in the hospitality industry. Sometimes a small, secluded place is just right. At The Home Ranch you can enjoy lodge rooms or one of the handful of cabins, each with its own heated Jacuzzi. This is a favorite of city folks who long for fresh air and a ranch environment.

Such "rustic" seclusion is not inexpensive, but with the sensational food, good company, intimate atmosphere, and the personal attention provided by host Ken Jones, it's worth it. You can enjoy skiing, riding, fishing, hiking with the llamas kept on the ranch, swimming, and snowshoeing. Nearby you can river raft or take flight in a hot air balloon. Discover this place before everyone else does!

You will fly to Steamboat Springs via Denver and the ranch staff will pick you up. The accommodations have varying prices, from $300 to $450 per person, per night, including all meals and activities.

Crescent H Ranch
Jackson Hole, WY

or

Firehole Ranch
West Yellowstone, MT

mailing address:
Rivermeadows
PO Box 347
Wilson, WY 83014
(307) 733-3674
(307) 733-2841

Crescent H Ranch and its sister, Firehole Ranch, are operated by the Rivermeadows properties. They offer superb guided fly-fishing and even instruction if you want it (ask about their schools). You also can choose a "ranch" vacation that includes horseback riding, hiking, boating, tennis, swimming, and fishing. Each property has slightly different options, depending on the facilities.

Nearby you can find rodeos, white water rafting, golf, national park tours, and shopping.

Western-style meals, from creekside cowboy breakfasts to authentic barbecues, are plentiful and satisfying. The accommodations are of the homey log cabin variety. Use your trip as a chance to see if you would like to own a home on the Crescent H Ranch.

Prices are about $200 per person, per night, which includes your lodging, meals, and all activities. Certain package plans, such as the fly-fishing school, are more. Jackson Hole is the nearest major airport.

Old West Dude Ranch Vacations
Division of American Wilderness Experience
PO Box 1486
Boulder, CO 80306
(303) 494-2992 (in Colorado)
800-444-DUDE

If you don't know which ranch experience would be just right for you, turn to the experts at Old West Dude Ranch Vacations. Representing 29 ranches in Montana, Wyoming, Colorado, and Arizona, these professionals will match you with the ranch that has the amenities, spirit, style, and price range that you are looking for. You can choose to stay in a cabin or a lodge, plus you can decide which activities are most appealing to you. Old West helps take the guesswork out of planning your trip. These are one-price vacations that include accommodations, meals, and all of the extras. And here's a plus: they will tell you the altitude of the ranch you select, in case that makes a difference to your health.

Skiing

Age is no impediment to the avid skier. And even if you have just decided to take up the sport, you will find excellent instructors, slopes that match your ability, resorts with the accommodations you want, and people you will enjoy.

As with all of the sections of this book, you will find organizations and accommodations that already cater to the 50+ market. The listings are not exhaustive but highly selective, to give you some excellent choices as you plan your adventures.

Organizations

Over the Hill Gang, International
6635 South Dayton, Suite 220
Englewood, CO 80111
(303) 790-2724

Back in the seventies, some ski instructors in Colorado noticed that many experienced skiers were no longer on the slopes. To lure them back they organized the Over the Hill Gang, which caters to skiers over 50. Today approximately 1,500 members participate in skiing trips organized through 16 "gangs" across the country. Off-season, members may be found drifting across the countryside in a hot air balloon, soaring in sail planes, or rafting down some white water river.

Boasting such famous members as President Gerald Ford, this group is made up of individuals who have both the means and the leisure time to participate in the many local, national, and international events planned throughout the year. The oldest member is 94 and the median age is 58. There's plenty of opportunity to meet people and make friends.

There's a $25 international membership fee plus local membership dues, as determined by the individual gang.

70+ Ski Club
104 East Side Drive
Ballston Lake, NY 12019
(518) 399-5458

In 1977, writer-broadcaster Lloyd T. Lambert was approached by a number of retired skiers who had all but given up the sport because they were on fixed incomes. Lambert arranged discounts with 30 area resorts to serve the charter membership of 34 skiers.

Today the group travels to ski resorts in

Switzerland, Argentina, New Zealand, Austria, and France as well as the many domestic ski areas.

The group, some with artificial hips and knees, some recovering from bypass surgery and some in their late eighties and nineties, supports the U.S. Ski Team Fund. The organization is limited to downhill skiers — no racers or cross-country skiers.

A lifetime membership is $5; overseas membership is $15 in U.S. funds. Members receive a card, a jacket patch, and a listing of ski areas offering free lift tickets or discounted rates. You must be an active downhill skier who can prove your age.

Association of Stratton Senior Skiers
Stratton Mountain, VT 05155
(802) 297-2200

This ski area provides a number of benefits to senior skiers. A school called Club 62 Plus provides instruction on designated dates throughout the season. For skiers 62 to 69, a modest annual membership provides half-price daily lift tickets or season passes. There is also a special Super Seniors membership price for those 70+ or older, which includes a free Stratton season pass.

Resorts

Big Sky Resort
PO Box 1
Big Sky, MT 59716
800-824-7767 (in Montana)
800-548-4486

This mountain hideaway was started by the late Chet Huntley to fulfill a dream of the perfect skiing resort. With both Yellowstone National Park and the Spanish Peaks Wilderness Area as neighbors, guests can revel in an undisturbed, carefully nurtured natural wonderland.

In the winter skiers quickly reach the slopes via two gondolas and five chair lifts. With this capacity, lines are virtually nonexistent. There are 55 miles of skiing on 40 trails to suit novices and experts alike. The ski school gives classes to beginners and pointers to experts. You also can enjoy skating, snowmobiling, cross-country skiing, and plenty of après-everything activities.

During the summer the resort provides golf, tennis, fishing, swimming, horseback riding, hiking, and lawn games. For the adventurous there's white water rafting.

The Huntley Lodge and a variety of condominiums provide cozy accommodations.

Air transportation is available by major airlines to Bozeman, Montana. Then you can rent a car for the 43-mile drive to Big Sky. With quad occupancy you can stay at Big Sky for less than $50 a person, but the accommodations can go up to around $125 or more per night (single), depending on what you choose.

Snowbird Ski and Summer Resort
Snowbird, UT 84092
800-453-3000

When you want to get skiing fast, you want an accessible resort. Snowbird is a mere 25 miles from Salt Lake City. With an average of 500 inches of snow annually and great skiing from mid-November till mid-June, this could become a favorite spot for a quick weekend getaway or for a week-long vacation.

There are plenty of lifts to keep lines to a minimum. Instructors are on hand to help skiers at all levels. The runs are beautiful, covering 1,900 acres. Even summers are fun, with concerts, festivals, and that famous clear Rocky Mountain air.

Heli-Skiing

You may be one of the advanced skiers who has been everywhere and tried the usual runs. Now you are looking for the ultimate skiing experience. There's only one alternative: heli-skiing. You and a small group of skiers will be transported by helicopter to mountain snowfields. You will ski through untouched powder on vertical runs ranging from 2,000 to 5,000 vertical feet.

In this backcountry powder paradise there's always the danger of an avalanche. For that reason, skiers are typically provided radio-signal devices to make skiers easy to locate, even if they are covered with snow.

These are pricey trips, owing to the expense of getting you to remote areas. However, you can count on a minimum number of runs or vertical feet. If weather prevents you from meeting your guaranteed minimum, you can expect a refund or a rain check. On the other hand, if you can squeeze in an extra run or two, you will be charged accordingly.

The specialized services that provide heli-skiing have a variety of packages and accommodations. Some have rustic lodges while others offer such amenities as Jacuzzis and saunas. Since each operator offers a different terrain requiring different levels of skill, discuss the details with the management before you make reservations.

On heli-skiing trips you can expect to meet adventurous and exciting companions who share your enthusiasm for the sport. Or take a group of your friends for an invigorating, unusual vacation.

Please be forewarned: these trips are strenuous. You should have a track record of toughness and endurance on the slopes. You should be in a regular exercise program that has built you up to the demands of this kind of skiing.

For the hardy skiier, the experience cannot be matched. For the foolhardy skiier, it can mean accident, injury, or death. Take into account the high altitudes that accompany this kind of skiing.

Canada Heli-Sports
PO Box 460
Whistler, British Columbia,
   Canada V0N 1B0
(604) 932-2070

Canadian Mountain Holidays
PO Box 1660
Banff, Alberta, Canada
   T0L 0C0
(403) 762-4531

Great Canadian Heli-Skiing
PO Box 1050
Golden, British Columbia,
   Canada V0A 1H0
(604) 344-2326

High Mountains Helicopter Skiing
PO Box 2217
Jackson, WY 83001
(307) 733-3274

Mike Wiegele Helicopter Skiing
PO Box 249
Banff, Alberta, Canada
T0L 0C0
(403) 762-5548
800-661-9170

Purcell Helicopter Skiing
PO Box 1530
Golden, British Columbia,
   Canada V0A 1H0
(604) 344-5410

Ruby Mountain Heli-Ski
PO Box 1192
Lamoille, NV 89828
(702) 753-6867

Sun Valley Helicopter Ski Guides
PO Box 978
Sun Valley, ID 83353
(208) 622-3108

Utah Powderbird Guides
PO Box 1760
Park City, UT 84060
(801) 649-9739

Walking and Cycling

So many people have taken up walking or bicycling as part of their normal fitness routine that it seems logical that those same people may enjoy organized walking or biking tours. These trips give you a chance to slow down enough to soak up the scenery and appreciate the charm of the quaint country villages and the back roads you might otherwise miss. Then, too, you will have the pleasure of joining like-minded companions your own age or younger and the time to forge friendships with people from across the country.

If you never have considered a walking or cycling tour because you feared it might be a strain, you should know that careful tour planners usually weave plenty of sightseeing and leisure time between the jaunts. They also have accompanying vans to haul your luggage and will take you and your cycle to the next point if you wish to skip a tour segment or cut one short. Most of the tours are designed to be active but not athletic; naturally, however, some terrains are more challenging than others. Individual trip descriptions are explicit about the nature of the tour.

It would be wise to precondition yourself with some cycling before your trip. Count on comfort-conscious bicycle seats; the companies don't want you chafing or aching. As always, if you have a question, ask when you make your reservation.

Typically the tours begin in an easy-to-reach location, near airports or other public transportation. Bikes usually are provided, but if you love your own, you can arrange to bring it. Most tour companies limit the number of participants to a civilized handful of under twenty or so, thus eliminating that annoying tour group feel.

American Youth Hostels
Box 37613
Washington, D.C. 20013-7613
(202) 783-6161

Forget the notion that the AYH is only for the chronologically young. Challenging and budget-conscious trips are available for the 50+ traveler as well. A typical trip might be an Alaskan bicycle tour. You must be able to manage on your own and be willing to pool your efforts with other guests in the hostels (dormitory-style lodgings or houses) along the way. Complete information is available from the office. Prices at hostels are low, $5 to $13 per night for members (membership is $15 for those over 55).

Backroads Bicycle Touring
1516 Fifth Street
Berkeley, CA 94710
(415) 527-1555
800-245-3874

Find out about the many tours this group organizes every year by requesting their extensive catalog. Many 50+ travelers take the regular trips to domestic and overseas destinations. However, the company also has two tours for those who may never have even considered cycling, thinking it would be too strenuous. There are six-day tours of the San Juan Islands in Puget Sound and weekend tours of Santa Ynez in southern California.

Costs for the trip range from about $100 per day on domestic tours to around $200 per day for international tours (subject to fluctuations in airfare). Lodging and bicycles are included. Your food also is included, except for one lunch and one dinner which are left free in the schedule so you can explore on your own.

Butterfield & Robinson
70 Bond Street, Suite 300
Toronto, Ontario, Canada M5B 1X3
(416) 864-1354
800-387-1147 (in the United States)
800-268-8415 (in Canada)

This company arranges tours for those who want the adventure of walking or bicycling through Italy, France, England, Ireland, Germany, Austria, and other countries, but don't want to rough it. Leisurely trips are appropriate, even for first-timers. (Only a couple of their trips are for conditioned athletes.) One of the most appealing tours is through the Loire Valley, where easy days of riding end with nights in beautiful châteaus.

These deluxe tours last from five to eight days with costs averaging $275 to $350 per day, including lodging, most meals, guides, bikes, tours, and tips.

International Bicycle Tours
7 Champlin Square
PO Box 754
Essex, CT 06426
(203) 767-7005
Fax: 203-767-3090

With tours specially designed for the 50+ traveler, this organization can take you to Holland, France, England, and even the Soviet

Union. The easiest routes are in Holland, where the land is flat. Trips are more challenging in England and reasonably strenuous in the Soviet Union. The tours are cosponsored by Elderhostel.

One tour group's average age was 67 and the group frequently has cyclists in their eighties.

Tours average approximately $100 per day and include ground transfers to and from the airport, bicycles, lodging with private bath or shower, breakfast and dinner daily, gratuities, taxes, and souvenir T-shirts.

Progressive Travels
Luxury Bicycling and Walking Tours
1932 First Avenue, Suite 1100
Seattle, WA 98101
(206) 443-4225
800-245-2229

Tour New Zealand, British Columbia, the Pacific Northwest, Ireland, Italy, France, or England for a close-up look at the culture as you cycle or walk through the countryside. There's time for individual exploration to complement the group activities. France is popular for international travelers, but the fairly recent addition of the Pacific Northwest itineraries has brought the appeal of luxury cycling tours closer to home.

These trips can accommodate any level of fitness. The upscale tours range from $200 to $375 per day and include lodging at the best available inns, châteaus, country houses, and hotels, most meals, bicycles, and guides.

Prevention Magazine Walking Club
33 East Minor Street
Emmaus, PA 18098
(215) 967-5171

Of the 50,000 active members of this, America's largest walking club, about half are 50+. The enthusiastic response of the members resulted in an annual All-American Walking Rally, plus numerous planned trips to the national forests across the country as well as other guided regional walking trips.

This high-energy group has members who have made a commitment to walking for life. They enthusiastically embrace the walking habit to improve their health (some are recovering from heart attacks and strokes). As a group they find a refreshing camaraderie when they meet for walking events throughout the year. Expect to meet lively, friendly, ready-for-adventure companions from all walks of life.

Skyland Holidays
1157 Melville
Vancouver, British Columbia,
   Canada V6E 2X5
(604) 685-6868

Call this company to book a cycling trip to the Orient. Japan is a country on wheels, so it is no surprise that a cycling tour is an obvious way to see the country at close range. Surprising to many is that the code of honor is so strong, you can leave your bicycle unlocked wherever you go. Cycling is interspersed with sightseeing during the 15-day tours.

This is one tour where you must bring your own bicycle. Trips are priced with airfare, most breakfasts and dinners, transfer fees, and various admissions. Expect to pay over $4,000 (from Vancouver) for this adventure, more from Toronto. Price changes based on fluctuating exchange rates and airline increases are to be expected.

The Wayfarers
172 Bellevue Avenue
Newport, RI 02840
(401) 849-5087

"Footloose through the countryside of England, Scotland, and Wales," they say, setting precisely the mood of their tours.

Every day's walk takes you 10 miles through charming villages, past thatched-roof houses and historic churches. You will stay in farmhouses, inns, or cottages. "Old friends" — those who book two or three consecutive walks — are offered a 5-percent discount. This is a relaxed, unpretentious way to see the area like a native.

Each trip is pleasantly paced over five days and six nights. Prices average about $200 per day and include lodging, all meals, and guides.

Accommodations

Historic Hotels, Landmark Homes, and B and Bs

Sometimes you want to step back in time, out of the mainstream, and enjoy the kind of hospitality that existed generations ago. Some travelers love to hop-scotch across the country trying out the delightful bed-and-breakfasts that open their doors to a handful of guests every night. Others enjoy luxuriating in the traditional atmosphere of a historic hotel. If this sounds like you, this section includes cross-references from other parts of the book as well as additional entries to point you to the handful of landmark resorts, historic estates, and charming B and Bs throughout the country.

A variety of packages are available at these hotels, many of which include meals, sports, and other activities. The lists of options are too extensive to elaborate here. Your various association memberships may provide a discount, usually on a space-available basis; be sure to clarify your discount at the time of booking.

One or two dollar signs follows each address in the next pages. In general, $ indicates rooms available for less than $100 per night; $$ includes rates from $100 on up. In cases where the nearest airport is not obvious from the name of the city, the closest major airport has been noted, together with the approximate driving time.

Boca Raton Resort and Club
501 East Camino Real
Boca Raton, FL 33432
(407) 395-3000
800-327-0101
Fax: 407-391-3183
$$

A landmark hotel, the original Cloister (see page 80), built in 1926, has a much-photographed Spanish architecture. During the winter months, historic tours of the hotel reveal intriguing details about its past. Today it still reigns as one of the leading luxury resorts on Florida's Gold Coast. It's a monument to traditional and gracious accommodations and service.

Boca Raton is served by the West Palm Beach or Fort Lauderdale airports, since it is 22 miles to either one.

Classic Inns by Treadway
180 Summit Avenue
Montvale, NJ 07645
800-TREADWAY
Fax: 201-666-1460

$

Over 75 years ago, Mr. L. G. Treadway opened his first inn with a commitment to good food, drink, and lodging. Today Treadway is America's oldest lodging chain of independently owned and operated properties. Many of the Treadway Inns carry the Classic Inns designation. These are charming historic mansions, inns, and lodges in delightful locales throughout the country.

Most offer bed-and-breakfast packages and free in-room freshly brewed coffee. There are other gracious touches, such as the original lemon soap in the bath and an apple from the front desk to take with you as you continue your journey.

With a Treadway directory in your hand, you can bypass ordinary lodgings and discover a new dimension of travel. The chain is rapidly growing to include inns and hotels in Canada, England, Europe, the Orient, and the Middle East.

A toll-free call will get you the directory. Although there is a certain sense of security in knowing that these inns answer to the main organization, you should take care when selecting your accommodations, as there is a wide variance in type and style of lodgings included under the Treadway umbrella.

The Cloister
100 First Street
Sea Island, GA 31561
(912) 638-3611
800-SEA-ISLAND
$$

The Cloister is the only hotel located on Sea Island and features five miles of private beach. Opened in 1928, it still offers traditional, yet casual, elegance and impeccable service. Another of the often-awarded traditional resorts of this country, the serene Spanish Mediterranean atmosphere offers a secluded, but complete, resort facility. Celebrities, dignitaries, and the socially prominent have made a generation-spanning tradition of visits to the Cloister.

The closest major airport is in Jacksonville, Florida, 70 miles away.

Dunlap House
635 Green Street
Gainesville, GA 30501
(404) 536-0200
$

Many are drawn to the beauty of historic Gainesville in the North Georgia Mountains (the location of the Georgia Mountains Center and the Quinlan Arts Center). When visiting, you may enjoy a classic luxury bed-and-breakfast inn, the Dunlap House. This property was restored in 1985 by a team of young businessmen who incorporated contemporary amenities while preserving the original charm.

Today 12 rooms provide the ultimate in gracious hospitality. Some rooms have fireplaces. Complimentary light refreshments are always available. Breakfast — a treat of fresh pastries, the morning paper, and rich coffee — can be enjoyed on the wide veranda.

The closest airport is in Atlanta, 70 miles away.

The Greenbrier
Station A
White Sulphur Springs, WV 24986
(304) 536-1110
800-624-6070
$$

This is truly a landmark resort nestled in the Allegheny Mountains of West Virginia. The hotel dates from 1778 and today is one of the most awarded, elegant facilities in the country. The employees outnumber the guests to assure old-fashioned southern hospitality.

The hotel is an impressive example of Georgian architecture. Yet with skillful renovation, the hotel offers every modern amenity, blended with stunning furnishings, antiques, and art.

The Roanoke airport is an hour away.

Grove Park Inn and Country Club
290 Macon Avenue
Asheville, NC 28804
(704) 252-2711
800-438-5800
$$

Grove Park Inn has been welcoming guests since the early part of this century. Listed in the National Register of Historical Places, it was built by a pharmacist as a healthful mountain retreat. It is also the place where such industrial leaders as Firestone, Edison, and their contemporaries would get together to brainstorm.

The imposing main stone building retains its original character, as does the country club, and you certainly will enjoy sitting on the veranda overlooking the misty hills. However, be prepared for some twentieth-century additions, including a high-powered convention and meeting facility and a fitness center. Fortunately, the look is still retained; the building is simply a whole lot bigger and more sprawling than it used to be.

Many drive through this mountain area, but Asheville's airport is served by major airlines.

The Homestead
Hot Springs, VA 24445
(703) 839-5500
800-542-5734 (in Virginia)
800-336-5771
$$

This mountain resort sprawls over 15,000 acres of beautiful Virginian countryside. In operation for over 200 years, this Georgian hotel has few peers in the historic tradition of grand old hotels. Families reunite for annual celebrations year after year.

The closest major airport is in Roanoke, Virginia, one and a half hours away.

Hotel Atop the Bellevue
1415 Chancellor Court
Philadelphia, PA 19102
800-222-0939
Fax: 215-732-8518
$$

The 172-room hotel has been reconstructed on the top seven floors of Philadelphia's landmark Bellevue building. The hotel is as elegant as you'd expect from a traditional luxury hotel. This is one of the elegant places where you can enjoy a proper English tea in the afternoon.

Lodge on the Desert
306 North Alvernon Way
PO Box 42500
Tucson, AZ 85733
(602) 325-3366
$

Think of an historic lodge and the first thing that comes to mind might be a grand old mansion on a colonial street in New England. Surprise! Here's a grand old lodge in the heart of Tucson. When built in 1936, the resort was an isolated retreat outside the town's borders. Guests could fly in, ". . . just 13 hours from New York and Washington, D.C. by the fast new planes." Air-conditioned trains brought guests from Chicago, California, and New Orleans.

Celebrities have escaped to blessed privacy behind the high adobe walls of the lodge. Even though the city has now grown up around the six-acre property, there is still a sense of seclusion. The hacienda buildings are furnished with authentic southwestern furnishings. Many of the 40 guest rooms have fireplaces. You can book for a short visit or stay for an extended period, forging lifelong friendships with other guests.

84

The Millcroft Inn
John Street
PO Box 89
Alton, Ontario, Canada L0N 1A0
(519) 941-8111
Fax: 416-857-6130
$$ (Canadian)

In the mid-1800s, Alton (an hour's drive north from Toronto) was a thriving community with two woolen mills, a saw mill, and other factories. The knitting mill, along with other riverside operations, had waterwheels in the Credit River to power its machinery.

When economic decline forced the knitting mill out of operation in the 1960s, it was renovated and opened in 1976 as Millcroft Inn. Today 22 charming guest accommodations, decorated with Canadian and European antiques, welcome guests to a placid life-style on 100 gorgeous acres. A renowned chef presides over the kitchen to provide excellent cuisine.

Mohonk Mountain House
New Paltz, NY 12561
(914) 255-1000
$$

This hotel, including the entire surrounding acreage, has been designated a national historic monument. The imposing structure has 276 guest accommodations, including actual single rooms for one person and bedrooms that share bath facilities, just as they did when the hotel first opened. Like many of the old, historic hotels, it has some appealing features, eccentric quirks, and quiet corners that simply cannot be duplicated in today's cookie-cutter hotels. Verandas draw guests outdoors in summer and 150 fireplaces warm them in winter. If you're a nature lover, this could be a playground for you.

The Albany airport is about one and one-half hours away and is the primary choice for air passengers.

Pinehurst Convention and Visitors Bureau
PO Box 2270
Southern Pines, NC 28388
800-346-5362

If you want to step back in time, you have to go only as far as Pinehurst to find a rich history with elegant traditions that live on today. Contact the Convention and Visitors Bureau at the toll-free number listed above for information about the variety of accommodations, from historic resorts to restored mansions offering bed and breakfast.

Visitors to this area either drive in or fly to Raleigh-Durham, 70 miles away.

Examples of the traditional hotels in the area include the Pinehurst Hotel and Country Club and the Mid Pines Resort:

Pinehurst Hotel and Country Club
PO Box 4000
Pinehurst, NC 28374
(919) 295-6811
800-672-4644 (in North Carolina)
$$

Opened in 1901, this legendary resort has a Victorian air but today's conveniences. This resort has seven world-class golf courses, a five-star tennis complex, pool, fishing, skeet and trap shooting, horseback riding, and even croquet. Enjoy great dining or linger over afternoon tea.

Mid Pines Resort
1010 Midland Road
Southern Pines, NC 28387
(919) 692-2114
800-323-2114 (East of the Mississippi River)
$$

Another generations-old resort, Mid Pines is casually elegant. The stately hotel features gracious southern decor. The Donald Ross golf course first opened in 1921.

Sterling Hotel
1300 H Street
Sacramento, CA 95814
(916) 448-1300
800-365-7660
$$

This old Victorian building has been renovated to provide twelve luxurious guest rooms. All feature Italian marble baths and Jacuzzis. Sleep in a canopy, four-poster, or sleigh bed. The hotel's restaurant, Chanterelle, is a highly rated dining spot that features California cuisine with a touch of French influence. During the week this is a popular stop for businesspeople, but weekends are for romantics.

Tides Inn
Irvington, VA 22480
(804) 438-5000
800-TIDES INN
$$

Many of the loyal guests who return season after season to the Tides Inn enjoy the unhurried, uncrowded atmosphere. Just 200 guests can enjoy the resort at any one time. This has promoted genuine and lasting friendships between the staff and guests.

Although as a resort the Tides Inn is casual during the day, guests dress for dinner as they might at their own country clubs. Many guests appreciate this often-forgotten gesture of civility.

Airports are one and a quarter to one and a half hours away in Richmond and Norfolk; a limousine will pick you up with 24-hour's notice.

Refer also to the "Alternative Accommodations" section, where a variation on the bed-and-breakfast concept is presented. The Evergreen Club provides inexpensive lodgings to a network of members who stay in one another's homes as they travel.

There are dozens of guides to regional historic inns and B and Bs. However, a good place to start looking is *Country Inns and Back Roads* or *Bed & Breakfast American Style,* by Jerry Levitin. The editors of *Old-House Journal* have published *The Old-House Lover's Guide to Inns* and *Bed & Breakfast Guest Houses.* The *Recommended Country Inns* series covers the whole country. *Bed & Breakfast USA,* by Betty Rundback and Nancy Kramer, is another option.

Resort Hotels With Your Health and Fitness in Mind

With health and fitness becoming more a

part of our everyday life, it stands to reason that our vacations and business travel would reflect this personal life-style. You may be less content to just go bake on a beach somewhere and call it a vacation. With our shifting attitudes, a new awareness of making vacations restful, but also rejuvenating, has resulted in a hotel and resort market poised to serve you in ways you may never have expected.

To help you plan your travel, the following pages contain a variety of listings and cross-references to help you find the precise kind of travel experience you want. All are geared to the active, health-conscious traveler.

This is not intended to be a comprehensive travel directory. The properties were hand-picked because of the health facilities and an existing satisfied 50+ clientele. Throughout the accommodations section you will see the symbols ¢, $, or $$, signifying budget (less than $50 per night), moderate ($50 to $100 per night), or deluxe prices ($100 or more per night). In the following section on resorts and spas, you will notice that routinely the properties carry $$ designations, meaning that rooms run at least $100 per night; some run several hundred dollars per night. You are paying for the privilege of staying at resorts with luxurious accommodations, excellent food, and extensive facilities, whether you use them or not.

The discounts you come to expect as a 50+ guest at a chain hotel rarely apply at these properties, but you can save money by choosing package plans or off-season dates. Rates will fluctuate with available room nights and discounts may apply when there are large blocks of rooms available. As always, ask. The kinds of places listed here appeal to the guest for whom price is a secondary consideration.

The geographical focus of this book is primarily on the United States. However, you will find the occasional listing for an outstanding property in Canada or the Caribbean.

If, like many others, you would like to dedicate some time to a tune-up of your body and mind, you might choose a destination from the first group of resorts, *wellness programs*. These have been specifically chosen because they have in-residence programs designed to help you lose weight, control stress, or develop a personal fitness and nutrition program.

Another type of residential program, the *spa retreat,* is designed to provide gentle ministrations to your face and body while giving attention to your health and fitness. Spa retreats differ from resident wellness programs only in that they offer more of a retreat from the world. They're oriented less toward the medical aspects of wellness and more toward pampering.

Active resort vacations may have extensive sports, recreational and fitness equipment, and even a professional staff to help you, but they do not have the extensive, defined programs of the previous groups. These are the resorts where there is always plenty to do, but you organize your own time as you please. There's less emphasis on classes, seminars, and workshops and, if there are professionals on staff, more emphasis on personal coaching.

For the avid golfer or tennis player, there is a *quick reference guide to golf and tennis,* a summary of the pertinent information, cross-referenced from the resort and spa material. This will give you quick access to the information you need to know if golf or tennis is the main reason you would select a particular vacation spot.

A list of hotels has been assembled under the *fitness-to-go* banner. These are hotels that have sufficient equipment, and in some cases professional staff, to help you stay with your fitness program while you're on the road. These hotels are, for the most part, the kind you might be staying at for a night or two while traveling, not one you would choose as a destination hotel.

It is interesting to note that while hoteliers are responsive to the demand for fitness-to-go, there's a wide difference in the facilities provided. Many have a modest assembly of basic equipment, such as stationary bikes and rowing machines. Others have state-of-the-art club-style facilities. Most have the requisite sauna–whirlpool–steam room setup. The listings give you an indication of what you can expect, but if you have specific equipment you require, double-check when you make reservations to make sure you'll have what you need.

For those who are conscious about their eating habits and wonder how to manage their diets on the road, look in the *nutrition on the road* section for the properties featuring low-cal, low-fat, low-salt menus or spa food. See the "Health and Safety" section (pages 383-394) for more information.

Wellness Programs: Rejuvenating Health With Medical Supervision

These properties sponsor serious wellness programs that can help you develop a new life-style of healthy habits while enjoying beautiful resort surroundings.

Because of the extensive medical testing

and evaluations, these programs are by nature costly (count on several hundred dollars per day — and up). However, participants routinely report that the life-changing effects are well worth the time and money invested. Package prices vary according to length of stay and service options selected. Meals usually are included, since most programs are designed to help you learn proper nutrition under supervision so you can carry on successfully at home. Don't expect discounts at these upscale resorts or for these specialized programs. You can save, however, by booking off-season.

The closest major airport is noted if it is not obvious from the address.

Aerobics Center Guest Lodge
12230 Preston Road
Dallas, TX 75230
(214) 386-4777
800-444-5192
$$

If you know anything about aerobics, you probably know the name Kenneth H. Cooper, M.D. Much of his pioneering work has taken place at his Dallas Aerobics Center. This beautiful property is a landscaped showplace in residential North Dallas. Driving past the grounds, you might see runners on a winding trail or a small group on the lawn stretching and bending in unison.

There are plans to fit any schedule: a 4-day "Wellness Weekend" or a 7-day or 13-day Aerobics Program for Total Well-Being. A comprehensive medical appraisal is followed by days filled with lectures and exercise. Field trips to nearby supermarkets and restaurants teach how to shop, cook, and dine out for heart health. Groups are small, for personal attention.

Travelers note: for reasonable day rates, you may use the facilities on a limited basis when passing through Dallas. Call (214) 233-4832 or 800-444-5764 for information.

Amelia Island Plantation
Amelia Island, FL 32034
(904) 261-6161
800-874-6878 (for reservations only)
$$

Located on 1,250 acres on a barrier island off Florida's Atlantic coast, Amelia Island Plantation has a pristine beach, outstanding golf, sensational tennis, and more. This is a quiet world where there's lots of activity.

The 45 holes of golf, 25 tennis courts, horseback riding, swimming, and fishing provide ample sports and recreation.

A health and fitness center on the property

includes exercise equipment, sauna, whirlpool, steam room, indoor-outdoor lap pool, and racquetball courts. In addition, the Baker International Wellness Center operates out of Amelia Island Plantation. An extension of Jacksonville's foremost cardiology clinic, the Baker International Wellness Center offers four- and seven-day programs that include a complete medical evaluation, nutritional counseling, stress management, and a personalized exercise program. The center also offers smoking cessation and weight-loss programs.

With selected real estate available, this is a possible location for a vacation to scout out a second home or a retirement home.

Amelia Island Plantation is 22 miles from the Jacksonville International Airport.

Canyon Ranch
8600 East Rockcliff
Tucson, AZ 85715
(602) 749-9000
800-742-9000
$$

Canyon Ranch
Bellefontaine
Kemble Street
Lenox, MA 01240
(413) 637-4100
800-326-7100
$$

Canyon Ranch has long been known as a front runner in the fitness vacation trend. A variety of programs is available at this coed ranch, some catering to the very fit, some to the stressed-out, some to the want-to-be-fit, and some even to chronically ill folks. For example, they have an individualized arthritis program sanctioned by the Southern Arizona Arthritis Association. You can even go to Canyon Ranch to stop smoking.

The menu of available services is so extensive, it takes a 36-page book to outline them all. As one of the most famous fitness spas, this property has everything you'd expect, plus a bit more. Though you certainly can be pampered at this ranch, the focus is on fitness. Be prepared to do some serious work to get the most from this retreat.

This is not an inexpensive resort, but that does not mean that it isn't a great bargain for those wishing to improve their health and fitness level. Summer rates are more economical. Typical stays range from 4 to 10 nights.

The hub of the resort is the historic clubhouse with the high-beamed ceilings and stone fireplaces. The spa is an impressive 62,000-square-foot complex filled with every imaginable facility, from gyms to a meditation room.

The Health and Healing Center houses the health professionals' offices. There are lighted tennis courts and golf nearby. If you take your health seriously but want to have fun, too, this is the place.

There is now a similar and equally impressive facility in the Berkshires.

The Greenbrier
Station A
White Sulphur Springs, WV 24986
(304) 536-1110
800-624-6070
$$

The Greenbrier offers it all for health, fitness, or pure pampering. This is the place to turn yourself over to the professionals and emerge after a weekend or a week (or longer), rejuvenated and refreshed.

For generations, guests have flocked to the Greenbrier to enjoy the mineral baths. In comfort and privacy, guests can luxuriate in mineral baths and whirlpools, feel the reviving effects of a Swiss shower or Scotch spray, then relax in a sauna or steam room. Professionals administer massages, facials, and body wraps. Full beauty treatments also are available.

The Greenbrier Clinic was established as a diagnostic health care center to provide wellness programs in the elegant Greenbrier resort setting. It's a perfect adjunct for the many corporate executive programs held at the property. A staff of internists, radiologists, and other health care professionals provide a comprehensive two-day health evaluation. Lifestyle guidance is provided once the diagnostic testing is complete. The intensive clinic program provides in two days what might take a week in another setting. There's follow-up for each participant.

For health and fitness, guests have the use of an impressive range of facilities. In the spa, there's an exercise studio and fitness equipment. Professionals provide evaluations and coaching. An elegant indoor pool is used for aquaerobic exercise classes, the outdoor pool for swimming and sunning.

Hiking trails are mapped out for guests, as are the jogging trails and parcourse trails, complete with fitness stations.

There are three 18-hole golf courses, 5 indoor and 15 outdoor tennis courts, and 2 heated platform tennis courts, plus bowling, fishing, horseback riding, and skiing . . . the list seems endless.

Greenbrier even sponsors a well-known cooking school, which teaches valuable how-tos, from wine selection to ethnic dishes. For those interested in fine food, this is a natural.

Loyal guests return year after year, particularly those who want to retreat from the world for the sake of their health and fitness.

The Roanoke airport is an hour away.

Hilton Head Health Institute
PO Box 7138
Hilton Head Island, SC 29938
(803) 785-7292
$$

The Hilton Head Health Institute is located at the Cottages in Shipyard Plantation resort. Guests stay in the luxurious cottage villas while participating in the residential Executive Health and Stress Management Program or the Weight Control Program. For relaxation, there's a pool, exercise facilities, the Shipyard golf and racquet clubs, and miles of private beach.

Yet, with all of the sports and fitness facilities, the institute does not take the "spa approach" to its programs. In both programs, which were developed by Dr. Peter M. Miller, a clinical psychologist and founder of the institute, the emphasis is on behavioral changes.

There are 6-, 12- and 26-day health-promotion and weight-control programs. Each begins with a full medical exam and personal health profile. Then an individualized exercise and nutritional program is designed. Classes, seminars, and workshops are balanced by exercise and free time to relax in the beautiful setting. While weight loss is an obvious goal, guests are taught how to make permanent changes in behavior so that they can maintain the loss. A special emphasis is on increasing the metabolism for maximum efficiency. A 12-month follow-up program for participants includes refresher courses.

Guests are given a medical exam and exercise stress test. A physician, psychologist, and health educator meet with each participant to establish health and fitness goals. Meals are created from low-fat, low-sodium, low-cholesterol menus with high complex carbohydrate content. Classes and workshops address key areas to improve health and decrease stress. A follow-up program tracks graduates.

These are serious programs designed to help individuals regain control over their lives and improve health for the long term.

The nearest major airport is Savannah, Georgia, an hour away.

Hyatt Regency Scottsdale
7500 Doubletree Ranch Road
Scottsdale, AZ 85258
(602) 991-3388
800-228-9000
$$

The Hyatt Regency in Scottsdale is a complete luxury resort with golf, tennis, a fitness center, and Hyatt's signature pools, fountains, and waterways.

Guests at the resort may participate in one-day to month-long personal fitness programs under the direction of Dr. Art Mollen of the Mollen Clinic. Unlike some other wellness programs, the Mollen Clinic is located at the resort but is separate from the hotel. Depending on the health evaluation and program you choose, you could spend anywhere from less than $200 to nearly a $1,000 with the clinic.

Dr. Mollen, a specialist in preventive medicine, is a well-known author, columnist, and lecturer on health and fitness. His program is not a quick fix but a realistic plan you can continue at home for better health and an increased level of fitness.

Participants are given individualized tests, including a body composition evaluation, a treadmill stress test, a fitness appraisal, and cholesterol screening. A personalized nutrition and fitness program is developed after the results are evaluated.

The resort provides the low-fat menus required on the Mollen Method. You'll be given fitness conditioning and body-building coaching by a personal trainer. Daily seminars cover a variety of health topics.

This is an excellent way to combine a vacation at an exclusive resort and a professional health and fitness course. The hotel is busiest from January to April and least expensive during the summer, so plan accordingly.

Palm-Aire Spa Resort
2501 Palm-Aire Drive North
Pompano Beach, FL 33069
(305) 972-3300
800-327-4960
$$

The Palm-Aire offers a two-week wellness program developed by Dr. Sherwood Gorbach of Tufts University School of Medicine. It encompasses nutrition, stress management, fitness, weight control, and self-esteem. The program is limited to 12 enrollees at a time for maximum effectiveness. Participants get first-class medical attention in a nonclinical, resort atmosphere. The program may be scheduled on a seasonal basis, so check to see when it is currently available.

Any guest can take advantage of the 40,000-square-foot complex with separate male and female facilities. All spa programs begin with a comprehensive evaluation so that a personalized routine can be designed. Exercise classes, equipment, a lap pool, a parcourse jogging track with exercise stations, and aquafloat pool exercises are available.

Choose from three modes of massage therapy — Swedish, shiatsu, or reflexology — a revitalizing aromatherapy, hydrotherapy, whirlpools, saunas, steam rooms, and contrast (hot/cold) pools.

Beauty treatments include facials, herbal wraps, scrubs, and more.

The week-long and four-day minispa vacations draw an incredible 80 percent return visit rate, attesting to the excellence of the program.

The resort boasts five 18-hole golf courses, 37 tennis courts, 6 pools, plus squash and racquetball. There's even a "golf fitness" alternative that combines golf and spa activities for fitness.

You can "take the spa home" with books, videos, cookbooks, water exercise equipment, and instruction sheets.

Fort Lauderdale has the closest major airport, about half an hour away.

Pritikin Longevity Centers
1910 Oceanfront Walk
Santa Monica, CA 90405
(213) 450-5433
800-421-0981 (in California)
800-421-9911
$$

Pritikin Longevity Centers now has locations in California, Pennsylvania, and Florida

(Miami). In addition, urban nonresident centers in cities across the country are either open already or under development.

This is the program that can change your life. The plan is definitely not from the "diet" mentality. You will learn new lifetime habits and new ways of eating in an intensive 13-day or 26-day program. There is only one goal: "to help you get healthy and stay healthy for the rest of your life."

There is a strong emphasis on exercise, which becomes a daily routine. Pritikin also offers counseling and lectures, so you will be armed with the information you need to know to carry out the program at home. A variety of Pritikin products is available in stores everywhere to help keep "graduates" on track.

Fly into Los Angeles or drive to the center.

Spa Retreats: Revitalization Through Pampering and Fitness

While these spas are concerned with your fitness, they also will pamper you with the body, skin, and spirit-renewing services that have made European spas a mecca for so many years. They will wrap you and massage you, cover you in herbal solutions, and generally work the kinks out while you enjoy the no-tension atmosphere.

With the many facilities these spas offer, virtually all qualify for the $$ designation, meaning that nightly rates will be at least $100. At many of these luxurious properties, the rates range up to several hundred dollars per night.

The closest major airport is noted if the address does not make it obvious.

If you would like help selecting a spa to fit your specific needs and budget, contact the agency Spa-Finders, your travel agent, or the spas described in the following pages.

Spa-Finders
(212) 475-1000
800-255-7727

Cliff Spa
Snowbird Ski and Summer Resort
Snowbird, UT 84092
(801) 742-2222, ext. 5900
$$

Operated as part of the larger Snowbird resort, the Cliff Spa offers a European-style experience. Schedule a half day or full day during your stay at Snowbird to add some pampering to your ski vacation. Or turn yourself over to the staff for a complete makeover with a one-night to seven-night spa vacation.

Visitors can use state-of-the-art exercise equipment, attend classes, and swim for fitness, then relax with a variety of hydrotherapy sessions, wraps, and beauty treatments.

Nutrition-conscious menus with low-fat, low-cholesterol dishes are available in the Aerie and the Spa Cafe.

Snowbird is just 31 miles from Salt Lake City.

The Cloister
100 First Street
Sea Island, GA 31561
(912) 638-3611
800-SEA-ISLAND
$$

The Cloister has a loyal clientele that returns year after year to enjoy the many resort facilities, the traditional, gracious accommodations, and the excellent service. This is one of the "old money" hotels that has served generations of the same families since it opened in 1928. It perpetuates some of the civilities lost in modern times (which are natural and comforting to some but may seem somewhat pretentious to others). For example, this traditional resort holds to such sometimes-forgotten touches as dressing for dinner; a dress guide is available to help you pack appropriately.

The spa offers a full range of services, from seaweed skin treatments to hydrotherapy, facials, and honey-almond "polish." The services include such treatments as aromatherapy, acupressure, and deep-sea scrubs. Total fitness evaluations and consultations, exercise on computerized machines, and classes also are offered.

When the Cloister opened in 1928, a modest 46 rooms were available. Today the award-winning resort sprawls over lush acreage and includes extensive sports and recreation options: golf, tennis, swimming, biking, sailing, fishing, skeet shooting, horseback riding, and more.

It's a fabulous choice for family get-togethers, especially for the holidays and special occasions, such as anniversaries.

The resort offers a full American plan, which includes three meals a day and many extras.

The closest major airport is in Jacksonville, Florida, 70 miles away.

Note: the Cloister does not accept credit cards.

Doral Resorts:

Doral Saturnia International Spa
8755 NW Thirty-sixth Street
Miami, FL 33178
800-247-8901 (in Florida)
800-331-7768
$$

Doral Ocean Beach Resort
4833 Collins Avenue
Miami, FL 33140
(305) 532-3600
$$

Doral Resort and Country Club
4400 Eighty-seventh Avenue NW
Miami, FL 33178
(305) 592-2000
Reservations for both Properties:
800-327-6334
800-FOR-A-TAN (in Florida)
$$

These three properties offer distinctly different, yet consistently luxurious, vacation options. With each, however, you will have access to the spa facilities.

Recognized as the most luxurious North American spa, the Saturnia has numerous options. The four-night and seven-night spa programs let you choose your emphasis: sports, health, or total image. Each package has a different slant to cater to your health and beauty needs. All use the exceptional spa facilities and selections from the long list of personal services.

Your accommodations will be in a luxury suite, and you'll enjoy gourmet spa dining. There are demonstrations and lectures to help you continue your spa experience at home. You will learn about the fat point system to control your weight. Special mother-daughter packages provide an ideal environment to nurture a relationship while renewing yourselves.

This is one of the spas that celebrities choose for a private escape, which should give you some insight into what you might expect.

Greenhouse Spa
PO Box 1144
Arlington, TX 76004
(817) 640-4000
$$

The Greenhouse has been renowned almost from the moment it opened in 1965. A project of the Great Southwest Corporation, Stanley Marcus (then president of Neiman-Marcus), and Charles of the Ritz, the spa was an instant hit with its women-only clientele.

In the past, this was a retreat for socialites; today's clientele represents a cross-section of women, including many professionals, who use the spa to revive themselves. There's a mystique about the place, largely due to its association with Neiman's; however, women no longer need to be dripping in diamonds or take along a week's worth of formal evening wear to feel appropriate.

This is a place for renewal. Because only thirty-nine guests can be accommodated at any one time, the atmosphere is always intimate and personal. Programs normally last a week, but four-day minispa plans are available on a space-available basis.

The emphasis is on health and beauty, with toning and conditioning exercises alternating with luscious beauty treatments.

Take note of the mother-daughter weeks planned each year. Time together can have a revitalizing effect on a relationship. When the emphasis can switch from work or family obligations to the important bond between mother and daughter, both can gain more than health and beauty during their stay.

Arlington is served by the Dallas–Fort Worth airport.

Gurney's Inn Resort and Spa
Old Montauk Highway
Montauk, NY 11954
(516) 668-2345
$$

Perhaps the least intimidating of the spa choices, this property offers a variety of plans, some of which are just over $100 per day. Among the packages available are three-day, two-night escapes and eight-day, seven-night rejuvenation weeks. Depending on the program selected, you can enjoy a prescribed course of therapy sessions and beauty treatments.

The spa is the only marinotherapeutic facility in North America. That simply means that water for the heated pool, Roman baths, and other hydrotherapy facilities is drawn from clear, deep seawater wells. The ocean-front accommodations put you right on the beach.

A special note: every Friday from 11 A.M. to 3 P.M., anyone, even nonguests, with an ID from a 50+ organization can use the facilities for a $5 fee.

Montauk is about two and a half hours from New York City and its two major airports. It also is served by the East Hampton Airport and the Montauk Airport.

Hotel Hana-Maui
PO Box 8
Hana Maui, Hawaii 96713
(808) 248-8211
800-321-HANA
Fax: 808-248-7202
$$

If you thought Hawaii had become over-developed, discover its pristine beauty again at the Hana-Maui on the eastern coast of Maui Island. With a dormant volcano separating Hana from the rest of the island, the quiet ranching village is secluded from the rest of Hawaii. This is a place of great natural beauty, caves, streams, hiking trails, and botanical gardens.

The one-story cottages offer privacy and luxury. You'll delight in the bleached hardwood floors, the Hawaiian art, and the authentic Hawaiian quilts on the beds. Enjoy tennis, swimming in the pool, strolling on the beach, the three-hole practice golf course, water sports, horseback riding, or jeep adventure tours.

The hotel has created a seven-day Hana Health and Fitness Retreat, held the first week of every month. Hikes to mountain pools and ancient temples balance the regular schedule of exercise and seminars. An elite group of only 12 guests may participate at any one session.

This unspoiled retreat is luxurious, with the kind of upper-range prices you'd expect from a remote, exclusive resort. But the experience available at Hana already may have been lost forever in virtually every other island resort locale.

Hana Airport serves the area; flights from other island airports arrive daily.

Maine Chance
5830 East Jean Avenue
Phoenix, AZ 85018
(602) 947-6365
$$

This all-female spa is a little oasis in the desert. Elizabeth Arden created this beauty resort to serve as an elegant retreat for women. The accent is on fitness and beauty, with calorie-controlled meals given the same beautiful presentation as the best gourmet meals. The spa has the atmosphere of a luxurious home filled with antiques and fine art.

Daytime clothes are provided. Plan to dress elegantly for dinner.

The six-day program includes exercise, heat treatments, skin care classes, facials, and massage. Contact Maine Chance directly for full details, as they do not use travel agents for bookings.

Pier House
One Duval Street
Key West, FL 33040
(305) 296-4600
800-432-3414 (in Florida)
$$

The mood is casual and the views are lovely in the tropical paradise called Key West. Pier House is right on a private beach, just steps from the historic old town. The addition of the Caribbean Spa Building gives the hotel the training equipment, sauna, whirlpool, and spa services for fitness and relaxation. Services are priced on an à la carte basis, so you pay only for those services you use. Packages also are available for a minispa experience.

There is a regional airport in Key West that provides service from Miami and other Florida airports.

Safety Harbor Spa & Fitness Center
105 North Bayshore Drive
Safety Harbor, FL 34695
(813) 726-1161
800-237-0155
$$

The mineral springs feeding this spa were discovered by Hernando DeSoto in the sixteenth century. The spa was built in 1926 to take advantage of what was promoted as the fountain of youth.

Today this spa, located near Tampa, is operated as a Lancôme Skin Care Institute.

Having recently undergone extensive renovations, this is now one of the most extensive facilities in the country.

Choose a short fitness weekend or a complete restorative week — numerous package plans are available. With the full American plan, spa services are à la carte. The many personal services are tempting: massage, a loofah salt-glow, herbal wraps, facials, hair treatments, beauty rituals. Plus there are 35 exercise classes daily, medical evaluations, tennis, golf at a nearby course, and, naturally, soaks in "the waters."

The institute takes a gentle approach, shunning aerobics, which is jarring and can lead to injury. They've added a new twist, box-aerobics, which uses the same training techniques as boxers use to get in shape. Many of the more than two hundred rooms overlook Tampa Bay.

If you're used to the best, you won't be disappointed.

Sonesta Beach Hotel and Spa
PO Box 1070
Hamilton 5, Bermuda
800-SONESTA
$$

Sonesta is a luxurious oceanfront resort featuring water sports, indoor and outdoor swimming pools, golf, six lighted Laykold tennis courts, and a complete health and beauty spa.

Guests have the option of prearranging the spa, minispa, tennis, golf, or scuba vacation of their choice. You can opt for a sports-and-fitness-only program or one that includes a massage, a facial, and other beauty rituals.

Shape magazine dubbed this place "one of the twelve best new spas" when it first opened in the late eighties.

Topnotch at Stowe Resort and Spa
PO Box 1458
Stowe, VT 05672
(802) 253-8585
800-451-8686
$–$$

Located in a pastoral mountain setting, this highly rated ski resort also offers superior spa facilities. Just 50 guests arc permitted to participate at any given time to assure personal attention. With the excellent outdoor facilities available, hiking, canoeing, and skiing may be integrated into your spa program. Room night prices include breakfast and dinner. Various spa packages are available. This is one of the most reasonably priced spa programs and a good choice for those who prefer the outdoors.

Burlington International Airport is about 35 minutes away.

Active Resort Vacations: Sports and Entertainment

Fill your days with golf, tennis, swimming, water sports, or even croquet and polo. Or maybe "active" to you means casinos or entertainment. Here are the resorts to satisfy your longing for a relaxed but lively vacation. Most properties listed are of award-winning quality, with prices to match ($$ means that prices begin at $100 per night). A few are moderately priced ($, or roughly between $50 and $100 per night) or inexpensive (¢, or under $50 per night). Depending on when you choose to travel, most resorts offer a package to include your accommodations and activities of choice. The closest major airport is noted when this is not clear from the address.

Boca Raton Resort and Club
501 East Camino Real
Boca Raton, FL 33429
(407) 395-3000
800-327-0101
Fax: 407-391-3183
$$

A 223-acre resort in the heart of Florida's Gold Coast, the Boca Raton is a traditional favorite of knowledgeable travelers. With a variety of luxurious accommodations, guests can choose course-side rooms or high-rise suites. Dating from 1926 — originally the Cloister — this resort has Spanish-style architecture, which has made it a landmark.

Play golf on either of two courses or tennis on one of 22 lighted courts. Take advantage of the full-service marina to go deep-sea fishing. A health club provides complete exercise and relaxation facilities. There are classes and a jogging track, two pools, and a private beach. Other activities include bicycling, croquet, and much more. Dining itself could be considered a major attraction at this elaborate resort complex.

January through April are the most pricey months; spring and fall are less expensive; you can get bargain rates in the summer. Reserve early for the popular snowbird winter season. Rates are European plan — in other words, no meals.

Boca Raton is served by both the West Palm Beach and Fort Lauderdale airports.

Carnival's Crystal Palace
Nassau, The Bahamas

U.S. address:
5225 NW 87th Avenue
Miami, FL 33178
800-222-7466
$

This qualifies as a moderately priced adventure, since your airfare and accommodations are included. Carnival built a reputation providing high-fun, low-cost cruises, and now, with their own charter planes, they fly travelers out of the Midwest and eastern states to their own hotel in Nassau. This is a high-volume charter operation — great for bargain hunters but possibly too "packaged" for the seasoned traveler.

A special "Play Day" package is just for you if you want a quick trip to Nassau while visiting Florida. For a moderate airfare, Carnival Air Lines will whisk you to the Crystal Palace. You will be given match-play chips and turned loose in the 30,000-square-foot casino. You also can play on the beach or in the pool. The one-day "Play Day" begins after breakfast and gets you back to Miami in time for dinner.

Cunard Hotels and Resorts
555 Fifth Avenue
New York, NY 10017
800-222-0939
$$

A small family of exceptional hotels reflects the attention to detail and gracious service that have built the reputation of the Cunard cruise lines. Look for Cunard to expand with choice properties in the United States and abroad. (Cunard operates the Watergate in Washington, D.C., and the Hotel Atop the Bellevue in Philadelphia.)

For an island escape, choose Paradise Village and Beach Club in the Barbados or Hotel La Toc and La Toc Suites in St. Lucia, West Indies. Both offer golf and tennis and watersports. Both are served by airports within a half-hour's drive.

If you like their ships, you'll love the Cunard hotels.

Doral Ocean Beach Resort
4833 Collins Avenue
Miami, FL 33140
(305) 532-3600
$$

Doral Resort and Country Club
4400 NW Eighty-seventh Avenue
Miami, FL 33178
(305) 592-2000
Reservations for both properties:
800-327-6334
800-FOR-A-TAN (in Florida)
$$

Choose either one of these elegant resorts and you have the best Florida has to offer. Both have sumptuous surroundings and attentive personnel. And while they share a common standard of excellence, they have distinctive characteristics.

An 18-floor tower dominates the Doral Ocean Beach Resort complex. You can step right out on Miami Beach from the pool terrace. The Doral Resort and Country Club, on the other hand, has a lower profile as it sprawls through lush tropical landscaping. There are 99 holes of golf for unparalleled golfing challenge.

With the Doral Saturnia International Spa Resort nearby, you can choose between the facilities of the various properties. If you like feeling privileged and pampered, this is one of those exclusive places that will suit you perfectly.

Grove Park Inn and Country Club
290 Macon Avenue
Asheville, NC 28804
(704) 252-2711
800-438-5800
$$

In the tradition of this nation's grand old hotels, Grove Park Inn was and continues to be one of the finest resorts in the country. Its main building, an impressive stone edifice built in 1912–13, has a commanding view of the Blue Ridge Mountains.

The resort has been extensively renovated and reflects its original grandeur. Substantial additions have been made, including a complete fitness center, but care has been taken to incorporate the old and new to preserve the traditional flavor of the property.

There are any number of packages to appeal to your special interests: jazz festivals; arts, crafts, and antiques; holiday celebrations; and more. Golf and tennis are among the favorite activities at the resort. This is another ideal multigeneration gathering place for holidays and vacations.

Although many wealthy guests stay at Grove Park Inn year after year, it is not the least bit intimidating to the first-time visitor, because with the addition of the huge meeting facilities, there are lots of first-time guests.

You do not have to be an insider to settle in quickly and take advantage of the facilities.

Asheville has its own airport.

The Homestead
Hot Springs, VA 24445
(703) 839-5500
800-542-5734 (in Virginia)
800-336-5771
$$

An American tradition, the Homestead has served generations of families for over 200 years. This is a place for reunions. The dining room has tables surrounded by grandparents, parents, and children, all enjoying the southern cooking the hotel serves best.

Built on hot springs, the grand old spa's focus has shifted from "taking the waters" to endless family gatherings at holidays and in between.

With 15,000 acres dotted with bathhouses, hiking and horseback riding trails, three golf courses, and (surprise) a ski run, there's always something to do.

The hotel has more than one thousand staff members to keep the place homey. Their success is measured by the 75-percent return visits rate by folks who have made the Homestead a private family tradition.

The closest major airport is in Roanoke, Virginia, one and a half hours away.

Loew's Ventana Canyon Resort
7000 North Resort Drive
Tucson, AZ 85725
(602) 299-2020
800-223-0888
$$

This elaborate resort is an impressive property that covers 94 acres in the foothills of the Santa Catalina Mountains. If you love the special beauty of the desert, this is an enchanting location — a real get-away-from-it-all kind of place.

The extensive facilities and professional staff permit guests to make their vacations a healthful time of rejuvenation. Guests can receive a fitness appraisal and have their body composition evaluated.

On weekdays, a morning workout alternates with the manager's morning run. Aerobics classes are held Monday through Saturday.

Golf and tennis are available, with professional instruction to improve your game. Swimming and exercise equipment also are available in the spa. The resort rents bicycles to the guests, or you can walk or run on the measured two-and-a-half-mile parcourse, complete with exercise stations, that rambles through the desert.

Beauty specialists provide a full range of services for men and women.

Lucayan Beach Resort Casino
Grand Bahama Island, The Bahamas

U.S. address:
KOGER CENTER
5225 NW 87th Avenue
Miami, FL 33178
(305) 591-2354
800-772-1227
Fax: 305-471-5658
$

For an exciting one-day jaunt to Grand Bahama, take a specially chartered Carnival Air Lines jet from Fort Lauderdale or West Palm Beach to this casino resort. This property has all of the expected amenities, from water sports to championship golf, but the real attraction is the 20,000-square-foot casino with a complimentary match-play coupon. You also will enjoy a complimentary lunch or dinner. Round-trip flights let you spend an afternoon or evening in Freeport and return to your Florida hotel, or you can make reservations to stay at the resort for several days. These are fun trips for a moderate price. Excursions may have the feeling of a group tour, which is ideal for some, annoying to others.

Makena Prince
5400 Makena Alanui
Kihei, Maui, Hawaii 96753
800-321-MAUI
Fax: 808-879-8763
$$

Every guest room at the Maui Prince resort property has a panoramic ocean view. This hotel offers a sports package that includes a choice of snorkeling, windsurfing, sailing on a catamaran, taking a helicopter tour, sightseeing by car, golf on the 18-hole course, or tennis on a five-star court.

The hotel is served by Kahului Airport, about 20 miles away.

Mohonk Mountain House
New Paltz, NY 12561
(914) 255-1000
$$

Mohonk Mountain House dates from the 1800s, when the Smiley family built the magnificent structure in the Shawangunk Mountains. Looking like a fantasy castle, this historic landmark is one of the grand resorts in the country.

Conceived as a quiet retreat, today's guests still can enjoy the natural beauty of the area.

The resort which can accommodate about 500 guests, offers traditionally decorated accommodations, many with working fireplaces. On the grounds, outstanding gardens and a greenhouse, museum, stables, and sports facilities gently invite visitors to relax and enjoy themselves at a slower pace. There is swimming, fishing, and boating on the lake in the summer and skiing and skating in the winter. There are tennis courts and a nine-hole golf course as well. A fitness center has equipment for exercise and classes.

Generation-spanning programs make this ideal for reunions. There's something for every age to enjoy. Ask about the special packages available.

The Albany airport is about one and a half hours away.

Opryland USA
2802 Opryland Drive
Nashville, TN 37214
(615) 889-6600
$-$$

For one-stop vacation fun, country music lovers can't find a better place than Opryland. You will find hotels, a theme park, the Grand Ole Opry, the General Jackson giant paddlewheel showboat on the Cumberland River, sightseeing, and more.

There are many lodging choices, both on and off the property. Budget buys will be off the premises but close by. Entrance fees to the park are remarkably reasonable.

Palm Beach Polo and Country Club
13198 Forest Hill Boulevard
West Palm Beach, FL 33414
(407) 798-7000
Fax: 407-798-7052
$$

Palm Beach has the requisite golf and tennis, but it also has polo, a distinct extra. The Equestrian Club is home to the Winter Equestrian Festival, and the jumping facilities are among the best in the world.

The 45 holes of golf challenge every level of skill. Tennis players can use any of the 24 courts — clay, grass, or hard surface. In addition, a swim and fitness center and two lighted championship croquet courts are available.

Dining is an event at the numerous restaurants. And, as you might expect, the guest accommodations are elegantly appointed studios, one-, two-, or three-bedroom residences. Candidly, this property caters to a wealthy clientele; it is considered a world-class resort for the most discriminating traveler. The socialite atmosphere may be too stiff for some, but for those who normally travel in these circles, it is quite perfect.

If you're looking for a luxurious resort or retirement home, consider the exclusive homes at this location. Villas, bungalows, and estates range from $200,000 to more than $1,000,000.

Palm Springs Desert Resorts
Convention and Visitors Bureau
Atrium Design Center
69-930 Hwy 111, Suite 201
Rancho Mirage, CA 92270
(619) 770-9000
¢–$$

In a stroke of marketing genius, as well as an intelligent consumer convenience, the resorts of Palm Springs offer an easy-to-comprehend area guide to plan your trip to this star-studded luxury community. Even though this upscale area is known as a playground for the wealthy, you can find moderately priced accommodations, even in the winter. Summer rates in some hotels and motels are even in the budget (¢ — under $50 per night) range.

As "the golf capital of the world," Palm Springs boasts over 100 golf courses. These range from gentle par three courses to championship courses that have confounded the pros. Many exclusive clubs are open only to members and guests. However, several honor reciprocal privileges with other clubs and others are open to the public.

You may want to know that there are 7,500 swimming pools and more than 500 tennis courts in the area. During the winter, there's cross-country skiing. Just for fun there are hot-air balloon rides, jeep trips, and more. The hectic social schedule includes a vast array of entertainment.

Don't forget that Palm Springs was named for the hot spring and mineral baths that still are available today.

A regional airport at Palm Springs serves the major airlines; however, connections can be difficult or inconvenient, so plan carefully. The Los Angeles airport is about two hours away.

Pinehurst Convention and Visitors Bureau
PO Box 2270
Southern Pines, NC 28388
800-346-5362
$–$$

Drenched in history, steeped in golfing tradition, and heavily laced with a Carolina-style country charm, this entire area is worth a leisurely visit.

The year's calendar is always filled with festivals and fairs.

More than 30 golf courses, many regarded

as the best anywhere, offer the golfer unlimited opportunities. The PGA/World Golf Hall of Fame is a testimony to the area's long-standing commitment to great golf.

But there's much more. Bicycling, horseback riding, polo, tennis, trap and skeet shooting, and other diversions are available. Plus there are many sightseeing attractions, wonderful shops, and excellent dining.

While the area offers economical lodging, there are also several historic lodges and quaint bed-and-breakfasts worth investigating. The Pinehurst Hotel and Country Club for example, has been in operation since 1901.

Visitors to this area either drive in or fly to Raleigh-Durham, 70 miles away.

Princess Hotels are located in several prime resort areas. Here's a sampling:

Acapulco Princess and Pierre Marques
Acapulco, Mexico
800-223-1818
$$

A sublime setting makes these neighboring hotels a wonderful choice for a relaxing resort vacation. If you can tear yourself away from the beautifully landscaped pools and lagoons or the fabulous beaches, there's golf, tennis, and water sports.

Scottsdale Princess
7575 East Princess Drive
Scottsdale, AZ 85255
800-223-1818
$$

A self-contained resort property, the Scottsdale Princess offers superb dining, golf, tennis, health club facilities, and a luxurious spa.

Bahamas Princess Resort and Casino
Box F 2623
Freeport, Grand Bahama Island, The Bahamas
800-233-1818
$$

With two golf courses, twelve tennis courts, pools, and a casino, there's action day and night. This elegant hotel is situated on a 2,500-acre island estate.

Southampton Princess
Box HM 11379
Hamilton 5, Bermuda HMFX
800-223-1818
$$

The English influence is felt at this luxury resort. Golf, tennis, swimming, and water sports fill the days; entertainment and fine dining fill the nights.

Saddlebrook
100 Saddlebrook Way
Wesley Chapel, FL 33543
(813) 973-1111
800-729-8383
$$

Situated on 480 acres in the countryside 25 miles north of Tampa International Airport, Saddlebrook is a residential and resort area with complete country club facilities. If you're looking for a place to settle in Florida, try Saddlebrook for a day, a week, or longer to see if you would like to buy one of the beautiful homes or homesites.

A consistent award winner, Saddlebrook offers a walking village concept with condominiums surrounding the amenities.

Two 18-hole championship golf courses and 37 tennis courts (27 Har-Tru, 10 Laykold), of which 5 are lighted, provide plenty of opportunity for play.

Sandestin
5500 U.S. Highway 98 East
Destin, FL 32541
(904) 267-8000
800-277-0800
Fax: 904-267-8222
$–$$

Year-round resort living is available to part- or full-time residents in rooms, suites, or custom-built homes. Golf, tennis, fishing, and water sports, plus seven and a half miles of waterfront, make this a picture-perfect Florida property.

The 2,600-acre complex features five restaurants, more than 30 shops, and much more. The management makes sure there are plenty of tournaments and entertainment throughout the year. Here's a note: Because of its location in the northern part of Florida, winter is the off-season, so rates are lower. Summer is the high season. With the largest Snowbird Club in America, this place hops throughout the winter. Make your plans accordingly.

The closest major airport is in Pensacola, Florida, about an hour away.

Sun City
137 South Pebble Beach Boulevard
Sun City Center, FL 33573
800-282-8040 (in Florida)
800-237-8200
$

If you want to use vacation time to scout for a retirement home, you could not invest your time better than to visit Sun City. Incredibly reasonable rates are offered for 5-

day, 4-night stays in the 140-room inn as an enticement to qualified prospective home buyers.

This town breaks just about every pre-conceived notion you may have about a retirement community. The folks are a lively bunch with a community that hums along smoothly, thanks to large doses of well-organized volunteerism. Retired professionals ply their trades for the benefit of everyone.

These people love life and one another. Drawn to the sun, they stay for the sense of community. The list of clubs and organizations is overwhelming. Plus there are 108 holes of golf, tennis, swimming, and fishing. Beaches are less than 10 minutes away.

Tampa International Airport is 25 miles away.

Golf and Tennis: A Quick Reference Guide

For the serious golfer and tennis player, here is a quick guide to the courses and courts. See the preceding sections; most of these properties are featured in one or more of the special interest sections. Here you will find the kinds of details that will help you choose your next vacation destination. Prices routinely will be in the deluxe range ($$ — more than $100 per day; some may be substantially more if you choose the most luxurious accommodations. A few are available for under $50 per night, designated a ¢). You may save money by inquiring about golf or tennis packages, which are promoted on a seasonal basis.

The closest airport is noted except for the major city destinations, which are obvious.

Boca Raton Resort and Club
501 East Camino Real
Boca Raton, FL 33429
(407) 395-3000
800-327-0101
Fax: 407-391-3183
$$

A popular Florida resort, Boca Raton attracts golfers with two 18-hole championship courses, a driving range, and a putting green.

Tennis buffs can play any of the 29 clay courts (some are lighted).

Boca Raton is served by both the West Palm Beach and Fort Lauderdale airports.

The Cloister
100 First Street
Sea Island, GA 31561
(912) 638-3611
800-SEA-ISLAND
$$

Golfing on the 36 holes of the Sea Island Golf Club will take you through the forests and cotton fields of the historic Retreat Plantation. Ask about senior tournaments.

Tennis is available on 18 courts.

Expect to meet traditional dress codes in the clubrooms as well as on the golf course and tennis courts.

The closest major airport is in Jacksonville, Florida, 70 miles away.

Doral Resort and Country Club
4400 NW Eighty-seventh Avenue
Miami, FL 33178
(305) 592-2000
800-327-6334
$$

Choose from ninety-nine holes of golf or play the famed Blue Monster course, considered one of the most difficult on the PGA Tour. The courses stretch over 2,400 acres and have more than 100 acres of lakes and 450 sand traps.

With five 18-hole courses plus a beginners'

course, 3 putting greens, and a lighted driving range, there's always some new challenge for the avid golfer.

Tennis is available on your choice of 15 courts, hard or clay surface.

The Greenbrier
Station A
White Sulphur Springs, WV 24986
(304) 536-1110
800-624-6070
$$

With three 18-hole championship golf courses, the Greenbrier offers a picturesque setting for challenging golf. The current course was designed by Jack Nicklaus; however, guests have been enjoying golf at the Greenbrier since 1914. The Lakeside course is open year-round. All three courses are open from spring through the fall.

Tennis players have a choice of 15 outdoor, 5 indoor, or 2 heated platform tennis courts.

The Roanoke airport is an hour away.

Grove Park Inn and Country Club
290 Macon Avenue
Asheville, NC 28804
(704) 252-2711
800-438-5800
$$

The sports activities here center around the historic country club. A challenging Donald Ross 18-hole course covers the rolling hills that spread gracefully before the inn.

There are nine tennis courts, three indoor and six outdoor, with clay or hard surfaces.

Asheville has its own airport with reasonably convenient connections.

Hyatt Regency Cerromar Beach
Road 693
Dorado, Puerto Rico 00645
800-228-9000
$$

Hyatt Dorado Beach
Call Box BB
Dorado, Puerto Rico 00645
800-228-9000
$$

These two hotels have a total of four 18-hole Robert Trent Jones courses.

Guests from both properties have access to 21 tennis courts.

The airport that has shuttle service is in San Juan, 45 minutes away.

Hyatt Regency Grand Cayman
Seven Mile Beach
Grand Cayman, Cayman Islands
West Indies
800-228-9000
$$

This hotel is part of the Britannia Golf and Beach Resort. Golfers can play this course one of two ways: 9-hole traditional or 18-hole Cayman-style. Cayman-style golf is played with specially designed golf balls, created by Jack Nicklaus and MacGregor, that travel only half the distance of conventional balls.

This property is just eight minutes from the airport.

Hyatt Regency Grand Cypress
1 Grand Cypress Boulevard
Orlando, FL 32819
800-228-9000
$$

The 18-hole par-72 course at this hotel was designed by Jack Nicklaus, who wanted it to be challenging yet fun.

The resort also features 11 tennis courts, 6 of them lighted.

Hyatt Regency Scottsdale
7500 East Doubletree Ranch Road
Scottsdale, AZ 85258
(602) 991-3388
800-228-9000
$$

This resort is part of the Gainey Ranch. Guests can walk from the main building to the Gainey Ranch Golf Club, which features a 27-hole golf course.

Tennis buffs will find eight Laykold tennis courts, four of which are lighted, and one grass court.

Loew's Ventana Canyon Resort
7000 North Resort Drive
Tucson, AZ 85725
(602) 299-2020
800-223-0888
$$

Golfers can play the 27-hole Fazio-designed PGA golf course or practice on the driving range and putting green.

Complete professional tennis training is available including private coaching and classes. The facilities include 10 lighted hard championship tennis courts, including one exhibition court.

Makena Prince
5400 Makena Alanui
Kihei, Maui, Hawaii 96753
800-321-MAUI
Fax: 808-879-8763
$$

The Makena Golf Course, hailed by *Golf Digest* as one of the top Hawaiian courses, is an 18-hole Robert Trent Jones design with sensational ocean views.

There are 6 tennis courts at the 5-star Makena Tennis Club.

The hotel is served by Kahului Airport about 20 miles away.

Meadowood Resort Hotel
900 Meadowood Lane
St. Helena, CA 94574
(707) 963-3646
800-458-8080 (in California)
$$

With the ambience of a country inn, Meadowood is an exclusive country club in California's Napa Valley wine country. The 9-green, 18-tee course has woods and creeks to challenge the best golfer.

Five championship tennis courts are protected by a natural bowl for wind-free matches. There's also a stadium court for exhibitions.

This property is about 90 miles from San Francisco; a small airport near the hotel serves private planes only.

Mohonk Mountain House
New Paltz, NY 12561
(914) 255-1000
$$

Golf is available on a Scottish-design course, augmented by a driving net and 18-hole putting green.

Tennis can be played on six clay courts. Platform tennis is available day or night on two lighted courts.

The Albany airport is about one and a half hours away and is the primary choice for air passengers.

Naples Bath & Tennis Club Resort
4995 Airport Road North
Naples, FL 33942
(813) 261-5777
$$

This tennis-oriented condominium hotel, located in a prestigious resort community, provides 25 fast-dry clay courts, 14 of which are lighted, plus 7 Laykold all-weather courts. A professional staff offers coaching and classes.

Oakwood Corporate Apartments
800-421-6654
¢–$

Most of these condominium communities across the country have tennis courts. These are 30-day rental properties.

Palm-Aire
2501 Palm-Aire Drive North
Pompano Beach, FL 33069
(305) 972-3300
800-327-4960
$$

Recognized as one of the top golf resorts in Florida, Palm-Aire has four 18-hole championship courses and one 18-hole executive course. Three courses have been designated by the *South Florida Business Journal* to be among the toughest in southern Florida.

There are 37 tennis courts.

Fort Lauderdale is just 20 minutes away.

Palm Beach Polo and Country Club
13198 Forest Hill Boulevard
West Palm Beach, FL 33414
(407) 798-7000
Fax: 407-798-7052
$$

This club offers 45 championship holes of golf. The designers were Ron Garl with Jerry

Pate, Pete Dye, and George Fazio.

Guests have a choice of playing surfaces for tennis; there are 20 clay courts, 2 grass courts, and 2 hard-surface courts.

Palm Springs Desert Resorts
Convention and Visitors Bureau
Atrium Design Center
69-930 Hwy 111, Suite 201
Rancho Mirage, CA 92270
(619) 770-9000
¢–$$

The site of many tournaments, Palm Springs boasts over 100 golf courses. Some are public, more are open only to members and guests, and many honor reciprocal agreements with other clubs.

For the complete overview of the golfing options, contact the area's Convention and Visitors Bureau. Some of the courses are legendary and each has its attraction, from devilish traps to elevated greens and water hazards.

There are more than 500 tennis courts in the area, providing endless game options.

There is a regional airport at Palm Springs that serves major airlines. However, connections can be difficult or inconvenient; plan carefully. The Los Angeles airport is about two hours away.

PGA National Resort
400 Avenue of the Champions
Palm Beach Gardens, FL 33418
(407) 627-2000
800-633-9150
$$

Billing itself as "the golfing capital of the world," this award-winning property is a haven for golfers and tennis players alike.

There are four courses, with a total of 72 holes of championship golf. Three courses were designed by the Fazio team; the other was designed by Arnold Palmer. Each has its own distinctive features for exciting play. The center for many tournaments, this resort provides a variety of challenges, even for the less-experienced player.

Tennis is available on 19 fast-dry clay courts.

Here's something different: there are five croquet courts, and professional instruction is available.

Pinehurst Convention and Visitors Bureau
PO Box 2270
Southern Pines, NC 28388
800-346-5362
¢–$$

A golfing mecca, Pinehurst has a long tradition of providing superb golfing facilities.

With more than 30 courses in the area, there's no end to the golfing enjoyment you can have.

Because the area, not just a single resort, is the attraction here, contact the Pinehurst Convention and Visitors Bureau for detailed information about the resort or golf courses that will fit your budget and your fantasy.

Visitors to this area either drive in or fly to Raleigh-Durham, 70 miles away.

The Pointe
7500 North Dreamy Draw Drive, Suite 215
Phoenix, AZ 85020
(602) 997-7777
800-876-4683
800-528-0428
$-$$

This prize-winning resort has three locations, and guests can be shuttled between properties to enjoy all of the facilities, including an 18-hole golf course and 25 lighted tennis courts.

Princess Hotels
800-223-1818
$-$$

Bahamas Princess
PO Box F-2623
Freeport, Grand Bahama Island, The Bahamas
800-223-1818
$–$$

Two championship courses provide exceptional play year-round on lush Wilson trademark greens at the Bahamas Princess.

Scottsdale Princess
7575 East Princess Drive
Scottsdale, AZ 85255
800-233-1818
$–$$

Two courses are adjacent to this resort operated by the Tournament Players Club, a subsidiary of the PGA Tour.

Southampton Princess
Box HM 11379
Hamilton 5, Bermuda HMFX
800-223-1818
$$

Golfers find this scenic course a challenge because of the ocean winds. For variety, there are a number of other courses nearby.

The hotel is 35 miles from the airport.

Saddlebrook
100 Saddlebrook Way
Wesley Chapel, FL 33543
(813) 973-1111
800-729-8383
$$

Two eighteen-hole championship courses were built by Arnold Palmer. With rolling greens and tall pines, the courses are a challenge.

Harry Hopman/Saddlebrook International Tennis is a teaching institution that has helped juniors through pros develop and refine their game. Innovative teaching techniques combined with small classes (no more than four students per instructor) give everyone a chance to advance quickly. Play on 27 Har-Tru and 10 Laykold courts. Five courts are lighted for night play.

Sandestin
5500 U.S. Highway 98 East
Destin, FL 32541
(904) 267-8000
800-277-0800
Fax: 904-267-8222
$–$$

Two golf courses designed by Tom Jackson offer exciting play on a total of 45 holes, while serious tennis players can enjoy Wimbledonstyle grass courts or hard-surface and Rubico courts, including two lighted courts. Both the Masters Academy of Golf and Masters Academy of Tennis provide intensive professional training during certain weeks of the year.

Tampa International Airport is 25 miles away.

Sheraton Tucson El Conquistador
10000 North Oracle Road
Tucson, AZ 85737
800-325-3535
$–$$

The 27-hole golf course features elevated tees, rugged desert fairways, double-tiered greens, and more.

Tennis is available on 16 lighted courts.

The Tides Inn
Irvington, VA 22480
(804) 438-5000
800-TIDES INN
$$

Tides Lodge
Irvington, VA 22480
(804) 438-6000
800-248-4337
$$

Golfers can enjoy 45 holes of golf on three courses: the 18-hole Golden Eagle Course, the 18-hole Tartan Course, and the 9-hole Executive Course. At the lodge, you are just minutes from your first tee. Golf cottages, complete with kitchenette, are available.

Tennis is available on fast-dry and all-weather courts.

Airports are one and a quarter to one and a half hours away in Richmond and Norfolk; a limousine will pick you up with 24-hours' notice.

Topnotch at Stowe Resort and Spa
PO Box 1458
Stowe, VT 05672
(802) 253-8585
800-451-8686
$–$$

This resort conducts a highly rated year-round tennis program.

Burlington International Airport is about 35 minutes away.

Westin La Paloma
3800 East Sunrise Drive
Tucson, AZ 85718
(602) 742-6000
800-228-3000
$–$$

The cultivated greens and desert fairways of the Jack Nicklaus course surround this resort.

Ten lighted courts, including four clay courts, are available for tennis.

The Golf Card
1137 East 2100 South
Salt Lake City, UT 84106
800-453-4260

Join this club and enjoy discounts and free play at more than 1,700 private and public courses across the nation with 24-hour advance reservation. Club cost is $75 single, $125 per couple.

Fitness on the Road

Leisure travelers are quickly learning what business travelers have known for some time: you don't have to leave your fitness program behind when you travel.

The information in this section is designed to help you find hotels that will provide the facilities you need to maintain your health program. These hotels are typically the city properties where you would stay en route, not necessarily the ones you would choose as a vacation destination. (See the earlier sections on spa retreats and active resort vacations for resort destinations.)

Because so many hotels are yielding to the consumer demand to have fitness equipment available, new facilities are being installed regularly. Hoteliers know that today's guests consider home-away-from-home a place where they can work fitness into the schedule regularly. However, just as with any trend, some properties are simply putting an exercise bike in a vacant room, building a tiny sauna, and calling that a fitness facility. It isn't until you put on your workout clothes and hike down to some dismal, out-of-the-way corner that you realize you are a victim of promotional hype.

The following properties provide the real thing; they are leading the industry with small but complete fitness rooms, complete health clubs in or close to the hotel, or, in a few cases, in-room equipment, such as a rowing machine or an exercise bicycle, for private workouts. This is not a complete list of those properties with suitable facilities (the list will keep growing), but it does represent hotels in both the moderate ($) and higher-priced ($$) ranges that have responded adequately to the public's demand for fitness on the road.

Courtyard Marriott
800-321-2211
$

Indoor and outdoor swimming pools, an exercise room, a sauna, and a steam bath are available.

Doral Hotels

Florida locations:
800-FOR-A-TAN (in Florida)
800-327-6334
$$

New York City locations:
800-223-5823
$$

The Doral Hotels have either a bicycle in your room or complimentary use of the fitness center.

Embassy Suites Hotels
800-EMBASSY
$

Depending on the location, you'll have a pool, a whirlpool, a sauna, and/or an exercise room. Alternatively, they may have health club facilities nearby. Exercise bicycles are available in approximately 10 percent of the suites. Ask about facilities when you call for reservations.

Fairmont Hotels
800-527-4727
$$

Fairmont Hotels have on-site fitness center facilities or a health club immediately adjacent to the hotel for moderate day rates ($10 to $15 a day).

Four Seasons Hotels
800-332-3442
$$

The Four Seasons hotels have varying but excellent facilities for fitness buffs, including such extras as horseback riding and archery, depending on the location.

Intercontinental Hotels
800-327-0200
$$

Fifty percent of Intercontinental hotel properties worldwide offer health facilities.

Hyatt Hotels
800-228-9000
$$

Virtually all Hyatt hotels offer some type of fitness facilities: pool, exercise equipment, jogging track, tennis courts, steam room, and sauna. The hotels in Philadelphia and Austin, Texas, feature bicycle trails on the grounds.

Hilton Hotels
800-HILTONS
$$

Facilities depend on the location. At Lake Arrowhead, California, for example, you can find skiing and a complete spa. At the Dallas-Fort Worth International Airport Hilton you can go horseback riding.

L'Ermitage Hotels
800-424-4443
$$

These hotels offer rooftop swimming, a mineral water spa, tennis, an exercise room, and in-room whirlpool tubs, depending on the location.

Loews Hotels
800-223-0888
$$

Although the facilities vary from location to location, all have fitness centers or an exercise bicycle that can be delivered to your room. Request yours when you make reservations.

Meridien Hotels
800-543-4300
$$

Most Meridien hotels feature an in-house fitness center or the use of a nearby club.

Oakwood Corporate Apartments
800-421-6654
$$

Most of the sixty-plus Oakwood locations nationwide have tennis courts, pools, saunas, a spa, and high-tech fitness centers.

Omni Hotels
800-THE-OMNI
$$

There are different facilities at every property. In Chicago, for example, runners are given maps, sweatbands, and Walkmans for their run through Lincoln Park. Otherwise guests can visit a nearby fitness club.

Sheraton Hotels and Resorts
800-325-3535
$$

Every hotel is different, and what is available at one hotel may not be available at another. Expect to find a fitness center with state-of-the-art equipment, pools, sauna, and whirlpool. Where feasible, the hotels offer tennis and golf. Some have extras, such as biking trails, scuba diving, and snorkeling.

Sonesta International
800-SONESTA
$$

This elite group of hotels offers spas and exercise rooms plus sports and recreation appropriate to the locale (water sports, golf, and so on).

Westin Hotels
800-228-3000
$$

At Westin hotels, athletic facilities are on-site or nearby. For example, in the Dallas Galleria location, you can even ice-skate indoors year-round at the ice garden in the mall. At other locations you can find golf, tennis, bicycling, hiking, and more.

Nutrition on the Road

If you're trying to lose weight despite your travel plans or just trying to maintain a heart-healthy diet, many hotels and restaurants are ready to help.

You already know most of the tricks you need for "defensive dining" while traveling.

- Ask for broiled or baked entrées instead of fried foods.
- Ask for sauces and salad dressings on the side.
- Try to get food in as natural a state as possible (with the exception of fresh fruits and

vegetables in Mexico or other off-shore locations, which could upset your stomach).

- Don't become a fast-food victim if you get trapped in an airport or other place where sugar and fat constitute the main ingredients of almost everything. Carry your own emergency pack with you, even on the plane — trail mix, herb teas, sugar substitute, salt substitute, individual packs of soup, packaged snacks from the health food store (for example, granola bars), low-sodium soy sauce, whole grain crackers, and fresh fruit. With the help of zip-top plastic bags and prepackaged individual servings, you can overcome flight delays or misplaced special-diet meals without a problem.

If you're traveling domestically, you may have a problem getting citrus over certain state lines. Overseas flights make even a sandwich a violation. In your suitcase you can carry plastic utensils plus your own traveling hot pot to make soups, coffee, or tea.

- For short stays, order fresh, uncut fruit up to your room. If you have time to scout, find a grocery store or health food store to stock up on fruit and juices.
- Book flights in advance so you can order special foods (see the specifics in the airline chapter).
- Contact your cruise ship in writing in ad-

vance to request special foods to fit your dietary needs. However, most ships today are adding low-cal or spa cuisine to their already extensive menus.

• Even fast-food restaurants now have somewhat healthy choices if you are careful not to douse low-cal, low-fat items with sauces, dips, and dressings.

There's no reason to sacrifice good flavor for good nutrition. Dine where four-star chefs prepare the food and you may learn a trick or two you can take home. With the chain hotels, make sure your destination hotel is a participant in the special-food programs listed in the following pages when you make reservations. If you just ask, most quality hotel restaurants will prepare your food however you want, regardless of what the menu says. Note, however, that special orders often take a bit longer, so be patient.

In addition to the hotels listed here, refer to the section on spa retreats. Among the first properties to recognize the importance of nutrition, spas devote the efforts of their star chefs to developing gourmet spa cuisine. They frequently give lessons on cooking and preparation techniques that will help you at home.

Doral Hotels and Resorts
800-223-5823 (for New York City properties)
800-223-5823 (for Florida properties)
800-FOR-A-TAN (in Florida)

Each Doral hotel and resort offers lighter entrées and healthful selections in its restaurants.

Hilton Hotels
800-HILTONS

Hilton's guests can enjoy "Fitness First" selections, with controlled calories, sodium, fat, cholesterol, and carbohydrates. You may find the counts on the menu, as you can at the Café Oasis at the Anaheim Hilton and Towers.

Embassy Suites Hotels
800-EMBASSY

The cooked-to-order breakfast and lunch buffets served at these hotels can be personally assembled to include the foods you want and ignore those extras you don't need.

Fairmont Hotels
800-527-4727

The fitness menu offered at Fairmont hotels is available in all restaurants as well as through room service. Gourmet selections meet the American Heart Association's eating-away-from-home dietary guidelines. The "Creative Cuisine" menu items are prepared with reduced fat and cholesterol with no added salt.

Four Seasons Hotels
800-332-3442

The Four Seasons' "Alternate Cuisine" was one of the first nutrition programs introduced by a hotel chain wishing to cater to health-conscious guests. The menu items are virtually indistinguishable from the regular gourmet dishes. Lunch items are less than 500 calories and dinners are less than 650 calories. Cholesterol and sodium levels are lower as well.

Hyatt Hotels
800-228-9000

Every Hyatt property features at least three "Perfect Balance" menu items in its all-purpose restaurant. These specially prepared dishes have fewer than 600 calories, and the food's composition is listed on the menu so that you can track protein, fat, and carbohydrates. Hyatt also has added low-alcohol and nonalcoholic beers, wines, and cocktails to its menus. You also will find more juice selections and a variety of bottled water. All of this is in response to higher consumer demand for alternatives, not just in food but in beverages, too.

L'Ermitage Hotels
800-424-4443

A nutrition-conscious diner could easily find many worthy selections on the normal menus at these hotels, from bran muffins in the morning to broiled swordfish at night. However, L'Ermitage's "Menu Minceur," or Light Cuisine, offers a variety of gourmet items created especially for the weight conscious.

Meridien Hotels
800-543-4300

Meridien's "cuisine dietetique gourmande" features low-cal ingredients and innovative cooking techniques to provide healthy fare in its restaurants.

Sheraton Hotels and Resorts
800-325-3535

The "Lighter Side" gourmet fare combined with menus filled with broiled or baked entrées, with sauces on the side, makes nutritional selections easy. Natural fruits, vegetables, herbal teas, mineral waters, and whole grain muffins are part of the nutrition-conscious menus.

Sonesta Hotels
800-SONESTA

Inquire when making reservations to see that your hotel offers "Healthy Alternatives" menu items or "Lighter Libations" low- and no-alcohol beverages.

Westin Hotels
800-228-3000
Start your day with freshly baked bran muffins, yogurt, seasonal fruits, granola. For lunch and dinner, select healthful salads, shakes, pasta, and other nutritious options as well as fresh seafood and mesquite-broiled entrées. Each hotel has its own versions of healthy alternatives.

Discounts

When planning a trip cross-country or staying near friends or family, it's often more important to find the hotels, motels, and inns that offer discounts than those with amenities you may never use. By stretching your budget, you can extend your visit or splurge on other travel expenses, such as a fabulous night out.

For your convenience, we have divided the list of accommodations for easy reference. The first group includes those wonderful, clean, dependable chains in the economy (¢ — less than $50 per night) to moderate

($ — $50 to $100 per night) price range. These properties operate coast-to-coast or within a specific region to give you a predictably nice room and friendly service. There rarely are surprises along the way, since even the independent operators working within a franchise system must meet stringent criteria to maintain their certification.

As the market demands have shifted, so have the amenities in these lodgings. Accommodations may come with such lovely extras as a free breakfast or other welcome touches. On the other hand, they may offer the no-frills approach to keep the price down. This may translate to such easy-to-tolerate economies as double beds rather than queen- or king-size, plastic glasses, and an area with vending machines to satisfy a snack attack instead of an all-night coffee shop or room service.

These are the places to choose when you are being cost conscious but want to make sure you have pleasant lodgings every night of your trip.

The second group includes upscale hotels ranging from high moderate pricing (the upper end of the $ range — $50 to $100 per night) to outright first-class luxury accommodations ($$ — more than $100 per night). There's no reason to ignore the discounts if they are available to give you more value for your travel dollar.

Prerequisites have been noted for your reference. Some properties honor AARP or other mature-market association discounts. Others have devised their own discount plans. Please check on the availability of the discounts at the property where you plan to stay. Most hotels have the option, even as part of a chain, to participate or not to participate in nationally advertised programs.

There are other ways to get discounts that could reap larger savings if you do some investigation:

- Don't forget to ask about other discounts available, such as special weekend packages or corporate discounts.
- Look for half-price coupon books that can save you big dollars. Make sure the restrictions match your plans.
- A club or association membership or a military or clergy ID may get you a better deal.
- Ask for a more modest room if cost is an object. If you're willing to let others occupy the rooms with a view, you could save by staying in a pleasant room without a view.
- Sometimes the hotel itself can extend cheaper rates than those posted in the computer at the 800 toll-free number.

- Negotiate when you arrive. You may not get an additional discount, but you could be given an upgrade. If the hotel's suites are empty, providing an upgrade for you is an inexpensive way to secure your good-will.

There is almost always a way to find a cheaper rate if you try!

ECONOMY TO MODERATELY PRICED LODGINGS

Contact the following chains for economy to moderately priced lodging. This particular group of hotels may also apply "luxury economy" or other descriptive phrases to their facilities to indicate that you get more than just inexpensive rooms. Many have upgraded their accommodations and some offer extras, such as complimentary coffee or a free breakfast.

Location and season can affect the price of a property, even within a given chain. The symbols ¢ (less than $50 per night) and $ ($50 to $100 per night) are given as guidelines only to help you select lodgings within your budget. Call for exact prices for the dates and locations you need.

Budgetel Inns
800-428-3438
¢–$
Age Minimum: 55
Discount: 10 percent at some locations
ID: Proof of age
Location: scattered in twenty states through-
out the South and the Midwest
Good to Know: Budgetel is an inexpensive
option. To avoid surprises, check on dis-
count availability when making reservations.

Country Hearth Inns
800-848-5767
¢–$
Age Minimum: 50
Discount: 10 percent
ID: proof of age
Location: Ohio, Indiana, Michigan, and Georgia
Good to Know: These low-cost bed-and-
breakfasts, located along interstate highways and in suburban areas, are just where
you are most likely to travel.

Days Inn
800-325-2525
800-241-5050 (to join September Days)
800-247-5152 (special September Days line)
¢–$

Age Minimum: 50

Discount: 15 to 50 percent on rooms and 10 percent on meals and gift shop purchases at participating properties; 10 percent to AARP members at most locations

ID: company-sponsored September Days; AARP

Location: United States, Canada, Mexico, the Netherlands, and more. Of the 250 participating properties, discounts can be found at Days Inn inns, hotels, suites, and Day Stops.

Good to Know: Days Inn was a pioneer in marketing to the 50+ market. The modest $12 annual membership fee provides discounts to local attractions, special trips and tours (including cruises), a newsletter, and, most notably, a full-service travel agency for members. Ask at a Days Inn or call for information. There's free flight insurance on all bookings. Consistent quality at several modest price levels provides a sense of confidence when traveling cross-country. Nonsmoking rooms are available.

Drury Inns
800-325-8300
¢–$
Age Minimum: AARP 50; otherwise 55
Discount: 10 percent

ID: AARP; proof of age
Location: continental United States
Good to Know: These budget motels offer
consistent quality at modest prices. Many
locations offer breakfast as part of the rate.
There is a frequent-stay program.

Econo Lodges of America
800-446-6900 (in the United States or Canada)
¢–$
Age Minimum: AARP 50; otherwise 55
Discount: 10 percent at most locations
ID: AARP; proof of age
Location: more than 460 locations in 43 states
and Canada
Good to Know: The budget-saving prices are
even better for members of the Econo
Traveler's Club. A free night is given for
every six nights spent at the same partici-
pating property in one year.

Economy Inns of America
800-826-0778
¢–$
Age Minimum: AARP 50; otherwise 55
Discount: 10 percent
ID: AARP; proof of age
Location: California, Florida, and Georgia
Good to Know: These budget-minded motels
are in key travel areas close to main high-

ways for easy access when traveling.

Friendship Inns International
800-453-4511 (in the United States and Canada)
¢
Age Minimum: AARP 50; otherwise 65
Discount: 10 percent
ID: AARP; proof of age
Location: nationwide in approximately 100
   cities
Good to Know: Consistent quality is available
   throughout the system at a moderate price.

Hampton Inns
800-HAMPTON
800-HTDD (TDD for the hearing impaired)
¢–$
Age Minimum: 50
Discount: Four-for-one price (four adults for
   a single price in one room)
ID: company-sponsored LifeStyle 50 program
   membership
Location: 145 locations nationwide
Good to Know: Apply for membership when
   you check in or call the toll-free number
   for an application. There is a visual alert system for the hearing impaired.

Harley Hotels
800-321-2323
$
Age Minimum: 50
Discount: 10 percent, except at New York City locations
ID: AARP
Location: 22 locations on the East Coast
Good to Know: This hotel chain is known for impeccable service, cleanliness, and attention to luxurious details. The Helmsley Hotels, the deluxe properties also operated by the same parent company, are distinctly deluxe in both style and price ($$).

Howard Johnson Lodges and Hotels
800-634-3464
¢–$
Age Minimum: AARP 50, Mature Outlook 55, and other recognized organizations; otherwise 59
Discount: 15 to 50 percent
ID: Organization membership card; proof of age
Location: United States, Canada, and Mexico
Good to Know: Even on heavily booked nights, you can receive a 15-percent discount. On off-nights you can enjoy a significant half-price discount. The Howard Johnson Road Rally allows you to collect

one "checkpoint" each night. Send three to the company and get coupons for additional savings on products and services. Plus there's a contest for significant prizes.

Inn Suites International
800-842-4242 (in the United States)
800-841-4242 (in Canada)
¢
Age Minimum: 55
Discount: 10 percent Monday through Thursday; 15 percent Friday through Sunday and holidays
ID: company-sponsored Silver Passport Program
Location: Arizona, California, and Canada
Good to Know: These attractive properties provide comfortable one- and two-bedroom suites. Breakfast and a morning newspaper are complimentary. The *Silver Passport News* is sent to members quarterly with updates and special information. Inquire at an Inn Suites or call for information.

Knights Inns and Arborgate Inns
800-722-7220
¢
Age Minimum: 55
Discount: 10 percent
ID: proof of age

Location: over two hundred locations throughout the Southeast

Good to Know: Even with budget-sensitive
room rates, accommodations are consistently
clean and comfortable.

La Quinta Inns
800-531-5900
¢–$

Age Minimum: AARP 50; Mature Outlook
55; others 55

Discount: 15 percent

ID: AARP; Mature Outlook; other memberships; proof of age

Location: approximately 200 throughout the
U.S., primarily in the South

Good to Know: Discounts may not be in effect
due to local events. The accommodations are
spacious for the moderate price.

LK Motels
800-282-5711
¢

Age Minimum: AARP 50; otherwise 55

Discount: 10 percent

ID: AARP; proof of age

Location: the Midwest

Good to Know: This is a budget chain with
a solid reputation for clean, comfortable
rooms. Properties are located along the in-

terstate highways as well as in smaller communities and suburbs.

Nendels Motor Inns
800-547-0106
¢–$
Age Minimum: 50 if an organization member; otherwise 60
Discount: 10 percent
ID: membership card; proof of age
Location: the Pacific Northwest and California
Good to Know: Some suites are available in this chain of motor inns. The Value Inn division offers more discounts.

Quality Inns and Hotels, Clarion Hotels and Resorts, Comfort Inns and Hotels, Rodeway Inns International, and Sleep Inns
800-221-2222
¢–$
Age Minimum: AARP 50; otherwise 60
Discount: 10 to 30 percent
ID: AARP; proof of age
Location: worldwide; Quality Inn is the largest American hotel chain, with twelve hundred participating properties
Good to Know: Quality Inn offers its 10 percent Prime Time discount any time. The Senior Saver lets you book ahead 30 days or more for a 30 percent discount with one

night's deposit (nonrefundable if cancelled less than 30 days in advance). The company has segmented its properties: Comfort Inns and Hotels provide luxury-budget lodging; Quality Inns and Hotels are mid-priced; Clarion Hotels and Resorts are in the deluxe motor lodge category; the relatively new Sleep Inns are for the economy minded. Travelers can enjoy a complimentary continental breakfast at more than 400 locations. Nonsmoking rooms are available.

Red Carpet Inns, Master Hosts Inns,
  and Scottish Inns
800-251-1962
¢–$
Age Minimum: AARP 50; otherwise 55
Discount: 10 percent
ID: AARP; proof of age
Location: United States and Canada
Good to Know: All of these hotel chains operate under the watchful corporate eye of Hospitality International. Discounts apply except for during high-demand times in localized areas.

Red Lion Inns
800-547-8010
$
Age Minimum: AARP 50

Discount: 20 percent
ID: AARP; other membership
Location: western states
Good to Know: Book ahead for their Prime
Rate, because blackout periods may apply.
Restaurants will give you 15 percent off foods
on the regular menu, except on holidays.

Red Roof Inns
800-843-7663
¢–$
Age Minimum: 60
Discount: 10 percent
ID: company-sponsored Redi-Card +60;
proof of age
Location: over 200 properties nationwide
Good to Know: The company thrives on its
back-to-basics approach. Rooms are consistent location to location. The Redi-Card
+60 has free membership and includes
such benefits as car rental discounts, room
discounts, other extras, and a quarterly
newsletter.

Shoney's Inns
800-222-2222
¢–$
Age Minimum: varies by property
Discount: 10 percent
ID: AARP; Mature Outlook; proof of age

Location: primarily in the South

Good to Know: Shoney's has a friendly family appeal. Each location is a franchise operation, so the discounts and terms may vary.

Super 8 Motels
800-843-1991
800-533-6634 (TDD toll-free reservation line)
¢
Age Minimum: AARP 50
Discount: varies by location
ID: AARP; other membership cards
Location: worldwide; 48 U.S. states, primarily in the Midwest and Northeast; and Canada
Good to Know: Super 8 enjoys an excellent reputation for friendliness, clean, attractive rooms, and convenient locations. More than 80 percent of the locations offer discounts to AARP and other organizations. Super 8 offers handicapped facilities.

Travelodge Inns and Viscount Hotels
800-255-3050
¢–$
Age Minimum: 50
Discount: 15 percent
ID: company-sponsored Classic Travel Club; any 50+ organization
Location: worldwide

Good to Know: Their new Classic Travel Club is attracting members from across the country. As Travelodge upgrades properties, people are discovering the "new" Travelodge. Club membership is one way people who have never tried the chain can enjoy its hospitality at a discount. Inquire at the property or call for information.

Vagabond Inns
800-522-1555
¢–$
Age Minimum: 55
Discount: up to 10 percent off a single room with no extra charges for up to three additional guests
ID: company-sponsored Club 55 ($10 annual fee)
Location: more than 40 properties, primarily in California, Nevada, Arizona, and New Mexico
Good to Know: Definitely a luxury version of moderately priced accommodations, Vagabond Inns provides lots of extras. There's a shower massage in every bath, free cable TV and movies, free continental breakfast, and more. Half of the rooms are reserved for nonsmokers. The 10th Night Free Program is available for frequent travelers. Inquire at the property or call for information.

UPSCALE AND LUXURY ACCOMMODATIONS

When you want to have a more luxurious stay, why not use the age-advantage discounts that are offered by some of the finest hotels and resorts? Review the ways to get your room rate to the minimum outlined at the beginning of this section on discounts. Even at the poshest resorts there's a special, a package, or a loophole that will give you better-than-regular rates. Even some of the high moderate locations have promoted rates for less than $50 a night in special packages.

Lodgings in this section generally range from high moderate, or closer to $100 per night, to luxurious rooms for several hundred dollars per night. Look for the symbols $ ($50 to $100 per night) and $$ (more than $100 per night) to guide you. Prices can differ dramatically within a given chain, simply because of location.

Aston Hotels and Resorts
800-92-ASTON (in the United States)
$–$$
Age Minimum: 62
Discount: 20 percent, free Budget Rent-a-Car
  every day of your stay; coupons for free
  meals and entry to local attractions

181

ID: company-sponsored Sun Club
Location: more than 30 properties in Hawaii
Good to Know: Anyone traveling with a Sun Club member also enjoys the free car and discounts. Inquire at the property or call for information.

Best Western
800-528-1234
$–$$
Age Minimum: 55
Discount: 10 percent
ID: proof of age
Location: worldwide
Good to Know: This is a chain of independently owned motels, so each property is different, but each meets a standard of quality. Advance reservations are required.

Colony Hotels and Resorts
800-367-6046
$–$$
Age Minimum: AARP 50; otherwise 59
Discount: AARP 25 percent; others 20 percent
ID: AARP; proof of age
Location: Hawaii and seven mainland states
Good to Know: This chain offers hotels, inns, resorts, and condominium rentals.

Compri Hotels
800-4-COMPRI
$–$$
Age Minimum: AARP 50; otherwise 60
Discount: 15 percent
ID: AARP; proof of age
Location: primarily California; scattered elsewhere in the United States
Good to Know: Guests share the Compri Club Room for socializing and cooked-to-order breakfast dining. In the evening, complimentary snacks are served. Impressive guest rooms have cable TV. Each hotel has an exercise room. Compri Hotels are great places to meet other travelers; friendly mingling is encouraged. Nonsmoking rooms are available.

Doral Hotels and Resorts
800-223-5823
$$
Age Minimum: 60
Discount: flat rates at New York hotels for Classics Club members
ID: proof of age
Location: New York City
Good to Know: These centrally located hotels are in some of New York's most appealing neighborhoods. They are beautifully decorated and appointed and provide a more in-

timate atmosphere for the city visitor. Call for information.

Doubletree Hotels
800-528-0444
$–$$
Age Minimum: 50
Discount: varies, but 15 percent is typical
ID: company-sponsored Silver Leaf Club; others
Location: primarily in the western and southwestern United States
Good to Know: These upscale hotels are frequently in city locations that are convenient to shopping and attractions or are desirable for guests needing access to offices and business parks. Call for club information.

Embassy Suites Hotels
800-EMBASSY
$–$$
Age Minimum: AARP 50; Silver SAAvers; otherwise 65
Discount: 10 percent
ID: AARP; NRTA NCSC; Silver SAAvers passport; proof of age
Location: continental United States and Hawaii
Good to Know: This hotel offers two-room suites that are roomy and comfortable, each

with a kitchenette. Breakfasts, lunches, and cocktails usually are served in the common area, a garden-like setting in the central lobby.

Hilton Hotels
800-HILTONS
800-492-3232 (enrollment Senior HHonors)
$–$$
Age Minimum: retired, 55; 60+ if working
Discount: 50 percent at participating hotels; 20 percent on meals at participating hotel restaurants
ID: 214-239-0511 company-sponsored Senior HHonors
Location: nationwide
Good to Know: You must be a member before you make reservations or check in. Membership is $45 per year or $75 for life. Members receive $25 certificates for every $300 spent.

Holiday Inns and Crowne Plaza
800-HOLIDAY
800-238-5544 (TDD for the hearing impaired)
$–$$
Age Minimum: 50
Discount: 10 to 20 percent on rooms; 10 percent on meals at participating hotels and restaurants

ID: AARP; Mature Outlook
Location: worldwide
Good to Know: Currently, Holiday Inns are completely restyling their programs designed for the 50+ guest. Contact them for the exciting new programs that are becoming available (and that may preclude the discounts outlined above).

Hyatt Hotels Worldwide
800-228-9000
$–$$
Age Minimum: varies
Discount: 10 to 50 percent or more, depending on the particular hotel
ID: varies
Location: worldwide
Good to Know: These luxury hotels and resorts have the kind of extras appreciated by experienced travelers, including fitness facilities, sports, and recreation. Each hotel sets its own policies, but a call to the central toll-free number should provide specific information on your destination hotel.

Marriott Hotels & Resorts
800-228-9290 (in the U.S. and Canada)
$–$$
Age Minimum: AARP 50; otherwise 62
Discount: 50 percent on rooms; 25 percent

on meals; 10 percent on gift shop purchases

ID: AARP; proof of age

Location: nationwide

Good to Know: The Leisurelife Program lets you extend your travel benefits to other traveling companions (up to eight in two rooms). Marriotts are going through extensive renovations and upgrades to cater to a more sophisticated and discerning traveler.

Oakwood Corporate Apartments

800-421-6654 (special seniors line)

¢–$

Age Minimum: 55

Discount: 33 percent (in winter only)

ID: proof of age

Location: more than 60 nationwide

Good to Know: Oakwood offers 30-day rentals for seniors. The prices would qualify as moderate if you were renting by the day, but since the lodgings are upscale, the properties are included in this section. The condominiums are furnished to the last towel for your convenience. Most have recreational facilities, including tennis and fitness centers. Mixing with the other guests is easy in the clubhouse. Complimentary Sunday brunch is served to guests. This is a great option if you want to spend several weeks in one location.

Omni Hotels
800-THE-OMNI
$$
Age Minimum: AARP 50
Discount: 50 percent on rooms; 15 percent on meals (not on alcoholic beverages)
ID: AARP
Location: worldwide
Good to Know: These are elegant, contemporary hotels known for their excellent service. Plan to ask ahead of time for mature market discounts when you order food or check in. You will need to show your ID. Nonregistered guests also may dine in the Omni restaurants at the discounted price, but they are asked to dine before 7 P.M.

Radisson Hotel International
800-333-3333
$–$$
Age Minimum: 50 if a member of an organization; otherwise 65
Discount: 25 percent
ID: AARP or other membership; proof of age
Location: worldwide
Good to Know: Radisson will extend your discount to your roommates, regardless of age. This hotel chain features luxury accommodations and quality service. Adventure and special interest packages are available.

Ramada
800-228-2828
800-2-RAMADA
$–$$
Age Minimum: 50 if an organization member; otherwise 59
Discount: varies, but 25 percent is typical at participating hotels
ID: almost any recognized organization's membership card
Location: nationwide
Good to Know: The Best Years Program offers generous discounts; however, they are limited during certain times.

Sheraton Hotels
800-325-3535 (in the U.S. and Canada)
$–$$
Age Minimum: AARP 50; otherwise 60
Discount: 25 percent on any but the lowest-priced rooms at participating hotels
ID: AARP; proof of age
Location: worldwide
Good to Know: Discounts may have local peak-time restrictions. Ask for your discount when making reservations. Sheraton provides upscale, consistent accommodations and service domestically and outside the U.S.

Sonesta International Hotels
800-SONESTA
$$
Age Minimum: AARP 50
Discount: 10 to 15 percent
ID: AARP
Location: vacation destinations
Good to Know: This small, exclusive family of luxury hotels is in a number of prime winter escape locations. They cater to personal pampering.

Stouffer Hotels
800-HOTELS-1
$–$$
Age Minimum: 60; some honor AARP
Discount: up to 50 percent
ID: AARP; proof of age
Location: United States and Mexico
Good to Know: The Stouffer Great Years Program is a terrific deal, but the heavily discounted rooms are limited in availability. Make advance reservations. Many first-class properties, such as Stanford Court, San Francisco, and the Mayflower, Washington, D.C., are under the Stouffer banner.

Westin Hotels & Resorts
800-228-3000
$-$$
Age Minimum: varies
Discount: 20 to 50 percent
ID: depends on the hotel; United Airlines Silver Wings Plus
Location: worldwide
Good to Know: Every hotel can set its own policy, so ask and reserve in advance. In the absence of senior discounts, request other discounts, such as the United, corporate, or weekend rates.

Westmark Hotels
800-544-0970
$-$$
Age Minimum: 65
Discount: substantial off-season rates
ID: proof of age
Location: Alaska, Yukon Territories, and Canada
Good to Know: Westmark Avis car packages are available. This hotel chain is associated with both cruise and rail lines.

Alternative Accommodations

What could be nicer than to stay with friends along the way on your trip or to settle into your own apartment or home at your destination for several weeks or longer? There's something inherently comforting about the notion of staying in a home. There are a number of ways for you to enjoy a home on the road, and most can save you money while providing a warm, inviting place to stay.

HOME HOSTS: STAYING IN PRIVATE HOMES

The Evergreen Club
1926 South Pacific Coast Highway
Redondo Beach, CA 90277
(213) 540-9600

When you become a member of the Evergreen Club, you have access to a directory filled with nearly 500 listings of other members, who will open their homes to you and your spouse for a modest $15 per couple or $10 for a single. You get a night's accommodation and breakfast. By having their homes available for the occasional guest, members can make use of other people's guest rooms on their own travels. This club is reserved for those 50+ and provides many opportunities to meet new people. Hosts are not required to entertain you, nor are you obliged to spend extensive time with them. Nevertheless, many people have found compatible people with whom they have become friends.

The club is not an exchange insofar as you are never required to open your home at any time for a visitor — only when it is convenient to you. The Evergreen Club provides the kind of network people enjoyed in years past when friends (or friends of friends) provided hospitality to travelers. Members give rave reviews of the delightful travel experiences they have had. It is a wonderful way to stretch your travel dollars and expand your network of friends.

Annual membership dues are $50 for a couple, $40 for a single person.

Servas
US Servas Committee
11 John Street
New York, NY 10038
(212) 267-0252

This nonprofit organization was established to promote world peace and international goodwill. You will arrange your own accommodations with participants. There is no cost beyond the $45 tax-deductible donation. You will have the opportunity to open your home to visitors as well, but you are not required to act as a host. Screening includes references and an interview. Send a self-addressed, stamped business-size envelope for information.

HOUSE SWAPPING

An inexpensive way to visit another place, but one that requires some careful logistics, is the house swap. You and another family simply exchange homes for the period of your vacation. Unless you know someone in the city or country where you want to be, it is usually better to trust an agency that specializes in house swaps. Or use one of the directories that allow you to contact other house swappers directly.

These agencies arrange swaps and rentals through their offices or via directories:

At Home Abroad
Sutton Town House
405 E. 56th Street Suite 6-H
New York, NY 10022
(212) 421-9165

Home Exchange International
22713 Ventura Boulevard, Suite F
Woodland Hills, CA 91364
(818) 992-8990

Interservice Home Exchange
PO Box 87
Glen Echo, MD 20812
(301) 229-7567

This agency's directory, with about 1,000 listings, including yours, costs $24.

Vacation Exchange Club
PO Box 820
Haleiwa, Hawaii 96712
(808) 638-8747 (in Hawaii)
800-638-3841

This organization produces four directories per year including a domestic version and three international issues. There are about 10,000 members. With your $50 membership fee you get a listing in one directory. You will receive all four directories and the newsletters. There is a 20 percent age-related discount.

Villas International
71 West 23rd Street
New York, NY 10010
(212) 929-7585
800-221-2260
Fax: 212-727-0246

This agency has a large inventory of homes available — approximately 30,000, including numerous unusual properties, such as castles and châteaus. Choose a London flat, a Paris apartment or one of the other exciting properties. There are no fees for consultation.

HOME RENTALS

When you are planning a trip to a location and plan to stay for some time, it is more cost-effective and often more relaxing to settle into an apartment or home. AARP, Grand Circle Travel, and SAGA Holidays (see the chapter "Guided Tours: Land, Sea, and Air") are all capable of arranging apartment rentals for you. In addition, there are a number of services that specialize in renting people's empty homes, vacation homes, time-shares, or condos. Also refer to the Oakwood Corporate Apartments listing in the section on discounts on upscale and luxury accommodations (page 187).

Home rentals:
In the English Manner
PO Box 936
Alamo, CA 94507
(415) 935-7065

This company specializes in Wales, Ireland, Scotland and England. The properties they represent are upscale.

Condos in Mexico, Hawaii, and Palm Springs:
Creative Leisure
PO Box 750189
Petaluma, CA 94975-0189
(707) 778-1800 (in California)
800-426-6367

Home rentals:
Elysees-Concorde
9 rue Royale
Paris, France

Times shares in the United States, the Caribbean, Mexico, and Hawaii:
TRI West
4742 La Villa Marina, Suite A
Marina Del Rey, CA 90292
(213) 823-1200

Home rentals in Europe:
Untours
c/o Idyll Limited
Box 405
Media, PA 19063
(215) 565-5242
Fax: 215-565-5142

CAMPUS HOUSING

One of the most economical ways to travel is to utilize the clean, safe housing on college campuses. There may be time restrictions when school is in session, but you can hardly beat the prices when the space is available.

Campus Travel Service
PO Box 5007
Laguna Beach, CA 92652
(714) 720-3729

For a directory of campus accommodations at more than 650 universities worldwide (350 in the U.S.), send $13.00 (includes postage and handling) to the address above. Prices for college rooms range from $12 to $24 per night, and you can enjoy the many student activities, from film festivals to sports. In the U.S., you can stay at colleges in locations as picturesque as Florida, Hawaii, and the Pacific Northwest.

Overseas, you can visit London, Paris, Berlin, Copenhagen, Brussels, Amsterdam, Vienna, and other popular cities for an average of $18 per night. In England, $20 will get you a night's lodging and breakfast. The directory also has a wealth of travel resources listed that can enhance your travel while reducing your costs.

Campus Holidays USA
242 Bellevue Avenue
Upper Montclair, NJ 07043
800-526-2915

Tour Great Britain and Scotland staying in universities (or, if you choose, with families) for modest rates, which include some meals.

CASTLES AND CHÂTEAUS

In Europe and England, there are a number of truly elegant lodgings available. Sometimes it is hard to believe that these actually were once residences, but for a few nights you can call them home sweet châteaus. If these accommodations are appealing to you, contact the tourist board of the country you wish to visit (see the chapter on tourist bureaus) for information or speak to your travel agent about the lodgings available and the cost. France, Germany, Austria, Spain, and England all have wonderful options to feed your fantasies.

Hotel and Resort Hotlines

For those hotels with TDD lines, please refer to the chapter "The Handicapped Traveler." Please note that where toll-free numbers are listed, they are normally for reservations only. Some 800 numbers are exclusively for the use of out-of-state callers, while others are only for those calling within a state. Notations have been made where possible. If no notation follows the number, you should be able to call from anywhere in the country. If you have trouble due to a number change, call the 800 directory assistance operator at 800-555-1212. Your travel agent should be able to help you contact any of these companies so that you can secure brochures or make reservations.

Absaroka Ranch	(307) 455-2275
Alaska Sports Fishing Lodge Association	800-352-2003
Amelia Island Plantation	800-874-6878
American Youth Hostels	(202) 783-6161
Aston Hotels and Resorts	800-92-ASTON
Best Western	800-528-1234
Big Sky Resort	800-548-4486; 800-824-7767 (in Montana)
Boca Raton Resort and Club	800-327-0101
Budgetel Inns	800-428-3438
Canyon Ranch:	
Arizona	800-742-9000
Berkshires	800-326-7100

Carnival's Crystal Palace	800-222-7466
Classic Inns by Treadway	800-TREADWAY
C Lazy U Ranch	(303) 887-3344
Cliff Spa	(801) 742-2222, ext. 5900
The Cloister	800-SEA-ISLAND
Colony Hotels and Resorts	800-367-6046
Compri	800-4-COMPRI
Country Hearth	800-848-5767
Courtyard Marriott	800-321-2211
Cunard Hotels and Resorts	800-222-0939
Days Inn	800-325-2525; 800-241-5050 (to join September Days)
September Days line	800-247-5152 (reservations for September Days)
Doral Hotels and Resorts	
New York City properties	800-223-5823
in Florida	800-FOR-A-TAN
for Florida properties	800-327-6334
Doubletree Hotels	800-528-0444
Drury Inns	800-325-8300
Dunlap House	(404) 536-0200
Econo Lodges	800-446-6900
Economy Inns of America	800-826-0778

Embassy Suites	800-EMBASSY
Fairmont Hotels	800-527-4727
Falcon	(207) 990-4534; 800-825-8234
Four Seasons Hotels	800-332-3442
Friendship Inns	800-453-4511
The Greenbrier	(304) 536-1110; 800-624-6070
Greenhouse Spa	(817) 640-4000
Grove Park Inn and Country Club	800-438-5800
Gurney's Inn Resort and Spa	(516) 668-2345
Hampton Inns	800-HAMPTON
Harley Hotels	800-321-2323
Hilton Head Institute	(803) 785-7292
Hilton Hotels	800-HILTONS
Holiday Inns	800-HOLIDAY
The Home Ranch	(303) 879-1780 (in Colorado); 800-223-7094
The Homestead	800-542-5734 (in Virginia); 800-336-5771
Hotel Hana Maui	800-321-HANA
Howard Johnson	800-634-3464
Hyatt Hotels	800-228-9000

Inn Suites	800-842-4242; 800-841-4242 (in Canada)
Intercontinental Hotels	800-327-0200
King Salmon Lodge	(907) 277-3033
Knights Inns and Arborgate	800-722-7220
La Quinta Motor Inns	800-531-5900
Leen's Lodge	(207) 947-7284 (winter); (207) 796-5575 (summer)
L'Ermitage Hotels	800-424-4443
Loews	800-223-0888
LK Motels	800-282-5711
Lodge on the Desert	(602) 325-3366
Lucayan Beach Resort Casino	800-772-1227
Maine Chance	(602) 947-6365
Makena Resort	800-321-MAUI
Marriott Hotels and Resorts	800-228-9290
Meadowood	(707) 963-3646; 800-458-8080 (in California)
Meridien Hotels	800-543-4300
Mid Pines Resort	(919) 692-2114

Millcroft Inn	(519) 941-8111
Mohonk Mountain House	(914) 255-1000
Naples Bath and Tennis Club	(813) 261-5777
Nendels Motor Inns	800-547-0106
Oakwood Corporate Apartments	800-421-6654
Old West Dude Ranch Vacations	(303) 494-2992 (in Colorado); 800-444-DUDE
Omni Hotels	800-THE-OMNI
Opryland	(615) 889-6600
Palm Aire	800-327-4960
Palm Beach Polo and Country Club	(407) 798-7000
Palm Springs Desert Resorts	(619) 770-9000; 800-432-3414 (in Florida)
Pier House	(305) 296-4600
Pinehurst Area Convention and Visitors Bureau	800-346-5362
Pinehurst Hotel and Country Club	800-672-4644 (in North Carolina); 800-458-4711
The Pointe	800-876-4683

Princess Hotels	800-223-1818
Pritikin Longevity Center	800-421-0981 (in California); 800-421-9911
Quality Inns and Hotels, Clarion Hotels and Resorts, Comfort Inns and Hotels	800-221-2222
Radisson Hotels	800-333-3333
Ramada	800-2-RAMADA
Red Carpet Inns, Master Host Inns, and Scottish Inns	800-251-1962
Red Lion	800-547-8010
Red Roof Inns	800-843-7663
Rodeway Inns International	800-228-2000
Saddlebrook	(813) 973-1111; 800-729-8383
Safety Harbor Spa and Fitness Center	(813) 726-1161; 800-237-0155
Sandestin	800-277-0800
Sheraton Hotels and Resorts	800-325-3535
Shoney's Inns	800-222-2222
Snowbird Ski Resort	800-453-3000
Sonesta International	800-SONESTA

Spa Finders	800-255-7727
Sterling Hotel	800-365-7660
Stouffer Hotels	800-HOTELS-1
Sun City	800-282-8040
	(in Florida);
	800-237-8200
Super 8 Motels	800-843-1991
The Tides Inn	800-TIDES INN
The Tides Lodge	800-248-4337
Topnotch at Stowe Resort and Spa	802-253-8585; 800-451-8686
Travelodge Inns and Viscount	800-255-3050
Treadway — *see* Classic Inns	
Vagabond	800-522-1555
Watergate Hotel	800-424-2736
Westin Hotels	800-228-3000
Westmark Hotels	800-544-0970

When Getting There Is the Adventure

Cruises

Is there any adventure that brings to mind more images of luxurious leisure than a cruise? For many, a cruise is a once-in-a-lifetime event. For others, it's an annual pilgrimage to yet another group of exotic ports of call. Sometimes it's a series of minivacations to familiar, sunny destinations.

As a 50+ passenger, you are part of the cruising majority. This industry was built primarily to serve and please you. You are bound to find the amenities that fit your picture of the perfect vacation at sea. You can expect some welcome pampering, including the foods you want. At least one line sends guests a preference profile so that the ship will be sure to have your favorite brands of mineral water, snacks, or whatever. On most ships, the kitchen staff can provide for your special dietary needs if they have written notice several weeks in advance.

Looking for the ideal cruise takes some time

and study, however. What do you want? Fun and nightlife? A huge, 1,000-passenger floating city filled with round-the-clock activities? Would a smaller vessel with a group of just a hundred or so sailing companions suit you better? Do you want to learn something by attending shipboard seminars?

These and other considerations can make the difference between the perfect voyage or a disappointing investment of time and money. Just like hotels and resorts, cruise ships cater to different tastes. Your travel agent, one who knows both your preferences and the style of various cruises, can help with any questions. For the best service when shopping for cruises, make sure the agent you choose is one of the 20,000–plus members of the Cruise Lines International Association (CLIA). You can identify association members by the CLIA emblem on the window, in the yellow pages ad, or displayed in the office.

If you are planning your first cruise, you might appreciate the information contained in a booklet published by CLIA, *Cruising: Answers to Your Most Asked Questions,* which is available through your CLIA-affiliated travel agency. The information will help you ask your travel agent intelligent questions and get relevant answers. You can learn about shipboard dress codes, tipping, and other potentially sticky questions. Today many cruises are informal, but there is a certain "cruise culture" with its own customs, especially on international ships, which could make you nervous unless you know what to do.

Cruise prices vary considerably, although you can always count on your room, meals, and shipboard activities being included. Some also include airfare to reach the ship and land packages for your visits in foreign ports of call. As a guide to the relative cost of the cruises in this section, prices have been translated into economy ($, or up to $200 per day), moderate ($$, or $200 to $300 per day), and deluxe ($$$, $300 and up per day). In this way, even if the rates fluctuate — and they will — you can get a sense of the relative cost of the various cruise lines.

Be aware, however, that with the change of seasons or low occupancy, even the most deluxe cruises can become bargains overnight. (See the "Cruise Discounts" section, starting on page 251.) Also note that the lowest price on the deluxe ships and the highest price on the low-cost cruises may not be represented. These are guidelines only for typical costs.

Industry insiders have helped to make sure the consultants and cruise lines editorialized in this section are reputable. The hotline directory (starting on page 254), is intended to give you an idea of the many cruise options you have so that you can follow up directly or through your travel agent.

It should be no surprise that even some of the most lauded lines have had the occasional sailing that is beset with problems. Equipment failures, for example, can thwart the best-planned trip. Nevertheless, cruises are among the most delightful, reliable vacation experiences, providing that you have been matched properly.

Cruise Consultants

There are cruise consultants to help you locate the cruise that matches your personal travel profile. These skilled professionals will have you complete a personal questionnaire, give you evaluations of various cruise lines, and tell you about their own experiences as well as provide reports from other clients. Cruise consultants are simply a specialized breed of travel agents, so they provide their services free to you. The four consultants listed below — all CLIA members — provide toll-free numbers; you can arrange all of the details from your home. If you prefer to deal with a local agent, contact the National Association of Cruise Only Agents or check the yellow pages for those in your area with the CLIA designation.

National Association of Cruise Only Agents
PO Box 7209
Freeport, NY 11520
This association will provide a list of the cruise-only agents in your area if you send a self-addressed, stamped envelope with your request. To be a member of this association, an agency must sell only cruises and must have personnel who sail several times a year to be able to give personal reports on good cruise values. Because of the high volume these agencies provide for the cruise lines, they often have enough clout to negotiate good rates and extras that would not be available to you otherwise.

Landry and Kling
1390 South Dixie Highway, Suite 1207
Coral Gables, FL 33148
(305) 661-1880
800-448-9002 (in California)
800-431-4007
This was one of the first cruise consulting firms to match passengers with cruises by interest, budget, land excursions available, and other criteria. They also can provide advice

on tipping, clothing, and other helpful cruise information.

South Florida Cruises
3561 NW 53rd Court
Fort Lauderdale, FL 33309
(305) 739-SHIP
800-327-SHIP

This leading cruise agency provides consultations through its toll-free number seven days a week, including evenings. They offer savings of $300 to $1,500 per cabin, depending on availability. They also can help single travelers find a congenial cruise group.

Cruises of Distinction
460 Bloomfield Avenue
Montclair, NJ 07042
(201) 744-1331 (in New Jersey)
800-634-3445

You can get on this agency's mailing list for its free quarterly update of cruise information. They also can provide the Instant Notice Service for a $39 fee, applicable to your cruise price, which will provide information on the greater discounts available on soon-to-sail cruises.

International Cruise Center
250 Old Country Road
Mineola, NY 11501
(516) 747-8880
800-221-3254

The International Cruise Center can help you plan Volga, Danube, Adriatic, and Mediterranean cruises. If the idea of exploring Russia, Greece, Italy, or Yugoslavia (to name only a few destinations) fascinates you, contact these consultants.

Also refer to the "Motorcoach Tours" section (pages 283-290), since many experienced travel companies, including Joli Tours, Mayflower Tours, and Domenico, also handle cruises. Check into the cruises offered by Suddenly Single; see the "Solo Travel" section (pages 322 and 320-326, respectively).

Luxury Worldwide Cruises

There are what must be considered "classic" cruises. These long journeys by sea on elegant ships are known for their on-board opulence and exotic ports of call. These are the cruises that take you to the lands you have longed to see. You can explore different cultures and shop in local markets for bargains in silks, gold, silver, gems, and other treasures, just as the merchants did centuries ago. Then you can retreat, thankfully, to accommodations that provide amenities many of these port cities and towns could not begin to provide.

These are the kinds of cruises that gave birth to the term *posh* (port out, starboard home), when sailing was in its zenith. And posh they are! These are the cruise lines to consider when only the best will do. Although you may not have to surrender your American Express card at the gangplank, expect to pay top dollar for these unmatched adventures.

And if these seem too rich for your taste, get hooked on the notion of a cruise in the descriptions that follow. Then use the suggestions for cruising at a discount or choose one of the trips described later for just a few hundred dollars. You never need to miss out on exciting adventures that capture the imagination. Simply get creative about how to enjoy them!

Cunard Line
555 Fifth Avenue
New York, NY 10017
800-221-4770
$$-$$$

As the line that operates the legendary *Queen Elizabeth 2*, Cunard long ago secured its place among world-class cruise lines. The only ship to offer regular transatlantic crossings (we're a long way from the time when ships were *the* way to travel), Cunard is absolutely committed to exceptional service in sumptuous surroundings. Awarded top honors by anyone who's anyone in the industry, the *QE2* is, quite simply, the ship of choice for many sophisticated travelers. Maybe it's the telling details, such as a shipboard tuxedo shop, that sets this vessel apart.

If you plan to travel on this elegant "city at sea," you will find every amenity known to first-class travelers. Each of the four main restaurants aboard have international reputations of their own. You will sample cuisine from a variety of countries during specially selected International Food Bazaar evenings. You will have at your disposal a wine cellar with more than 20,000 selections. Midnight buffets are offered as well as midmorning bullion and afternoon tea service. And of course there's 24-hour room service, too.

The sports facilities occupy an entire deck and an on-board version of the famous Golden Door Spa. Use weight equipment, jog on the track, swim in any of the four pools, and relax in the Jacuzzis.

For recreation, there's great shopping, game centers (one for children, another for adults), a library, and a theater, plus VCRs in every first-class stateroom.

Every evening is glamorous, with entertainment in the Queen's Room, dancing, lounges, and a casino.

And here are some features you never imagined you'd find at sea: the world's only seagoing American Express Bank, direct-dial telephone service to anywhere in the world from every stateroom, an IBM computer learning center, a florist, a hospital, a kennel, and, to bring back the Benz, a 40-car garage.

But the *QE2* is only one of the Cunard line's great ships. This is the line famous for world cruises; aboard a Cunard ship, you can visit every continent in about 100 days. Or visit Europe and the Mediterranean, the Caribbean, or the Pacific. Like all international cruise lines, Cunard schedules both summer and winter itineraries, sometimes to old, familiar ports, sometimes to new ones. You can always be sure, however, that your enjoyment is paramount to these experts. Depending on the cruise, you could schedule a voyage as short as a week and as long as three months.

Cunard has introduced some informal cruises at less-than-intimidating rates for those looking for high quality at consumer-conscious prices. To find out what is available, call the line directly via its toll-free number.

See also the information about spas at sea in the "Something Special Cruises" section (page 232-251).

Ocean Cruise Lines and Pearl Cruises
1510 SE 17th Street
Fort Lauderdale, FL 33316
(305) 764-3500
800-426-3588
$$–$$$

Ocean Cruise Lines and Pearl Cruises are favorites of the 50+ traveler for many reasons. Ocean Cruise Lines was formed in 1983 by a Swiss company specifically to assure a European tour operator first-class cruise accommodations in the Mediterranean. From those first cruises in the Mediterranean, the line expanded into Scandinavia, the Caribbean, and South America, gaining an excellent reputation. In 1987, the company acquired Pearl Cruises, which operates in the Orient.

Serving an upscale market, both lines consider themselves *the* cruise lines for land lovers. Typically a guest can combine pre- and post-cruise land packages and the cruise for an unforgettable experience. Itinerary planning is a specialty of the company as well. Since they serve a well-traveled clientele, cruises will intermix well-known ports of call at large cities with visits to lesser-known but charming and intriguing ports along the way.

The CruiseTour concept provides a complete, no-worries package that includes transatlantic flights, first-class hotels, sightseeing, and all baggage handling and transfers.

Ocean Cruise Lines will surprise you with the variety offered in its itineraries. You can enjoy ports from the Riviera to the Baltic capitals. The breadth and depth of the culture you see will expand your vacation into a floating lesson in history, art, and architecture. Among the many cruises available, you can find a classic European voyage that will give you the best Europe has to offer. There are transatlantic crossings as well for that not-to-be-missed ocean voyage.

Pearl Cruises are in demand simply because the line is the only one to offer year-round cruises to the Orient. The ship calls at ports in Thailand, Malaysia, the Philippines, China, Indonesia, Burma, and India. Pearl Cruises makes the visits more memorable by providing guest lecturers who bring insight and understanding of the cultures and countries.

Oceanic Cruises
c/o SMI Group
188 The Embarcadero, Suite 480
San Francisco, CA 94105
(415) 227-0781
800-545-5778
$$$

The first Japanese luxury ship, *Oceanic Grace*, was launched in 1989. There are 60 deluxe outside cabins and the cuisine is created from the freshest foods boarded at each port. The *Oceanic Grace* provides itineraries of 4 to 14 days that include several exotic ports of call.

Princess Cruises
(They prefer that you contact your travel agent.)
$–$$

This is the "Love Boat" cruise line that boasts both the facilities and the staff to make your cruise as memorable as you expect. Enjoy one of the popular European cruises, including routes to Scandinavia and Russia. There are also cruises to Alaska, perhaps today's favorite spot, and the Caribbean.

Your ship will envelop you in a world of luxury and splendor. Sweeping staircases, rich wood paneling, and elegant appointments throughout make this a sensuous environment.

In your stateroom, you will find spacious accommodations with lovely decor and storage space to spare. The *Royal Princess* is the only ship of its size to have all outside staterooms, so you can count on a good view.

As you would expect, there are fitness facilities, sensational dining, and a dazzling night-life.

Princess also is known for its Lecture Series at Sea, which includes renowned literary guests. Consult with your travel agent about which cruises may have this added feature.

Royal Viking Line
95 Merrick Way
Coral Gables, FL 33134
(305) 447-9660
800-422-8000
$$–$$$

These cruise experts do not issue just a cruise brochure, they have a hefty cruise "atlas" to describe the many sensational cruises they provide worldwide.

The characteristic Scandinavian efficiency, hospitality, and attention to detail are evident everywhere on the Royal Viking ships. A much-awarded line, Royal Viking harks back to the sailing traditions that have been lost along the way on some lines. Broad teak promenades, tireless attention by friendly staff members, staterooms with just enough extra room to accommodate you in comfort — you will know that this is one of the classics.

Royal Viking's cuisine has an international flavor but nods toward dishes favored in Scandinavia (Norwegian silver salmon, for example).

The cruises are grouped to appeal to the novice and the well-traveled alike. They offer appealing short getaways right on up to a 109-day world cruise. With this line, you can choose to visit the Americas, Asia, the South Pacific, or Europe. Like the other luxury liners, it's tough to know which is more fun — to be on the ship itself or to explore the intriguing ports of call. For those with a little more adventure in mind, Royal Viking has designed an Explorer Series, cruises that take in the most exotic ports.

On board, your days can begin with your usual health and fitness routine. Jog on the deck and exercise in the spa. Swim or simply bask in the sun. Enjoy the company of your sailing companions and visiting guest speakers, including renowned journalists, authors, and lecturers.

At night you will delight to the efforts of

nearly three dozen highly trained chefs. In fact, Royal Viking is the first cruise line to have been granted membership in Les Toque Blanches and the Master Chefs Institute. You will be attended by European-trained waiters who bring the strict service standards of the finest hotels with them. After dinner, prepare to ignite the romance in your life. Royal Viking provides nostalgic big band sounds for dancing.

Like its luxurious peers, Royal Viking transports you into a timeless cocoon, wrapping you up in the kind of pampered elegance that makes you forget the everyday world. You easily could picture yourself as an intrepid ocean voyager of a century or so ago, only you have contemporary services at hand. This will be a rare adventure.

Seabourn Cruise Line
55 Francisco Street
San Francisco, CA 94133
(415) 391-7444
800-351-9595
$$$

Another company that has built a reputation of uncompromising excellence is the Seabourn Cruise Line. Targeting the experienced and discriminating traveler, Seabourn's appeal is in its "new-generation" approach to sailing.

The ships are considerably smaller than the massive luxury liners you might expect, providing a more intimate atmosphere among passengers.

There is more elbow room in the bigger suites; comparably sized ships carry twice as many passengers! These suites have comfortable seating areas, bar, telephone, TV, and VCR. You can catch a "golden oldie" video on a quiet evening alone. The bathrooms are unheard of among cruise accommodations: twin sinks, shower-tub combinations, walk-in closets. You will become spoiled!

Entertainment on a Seabourn cruise leans more toward quiet piano music and reading from the selections in the library. Passengers tend to be more independent, more inclined to entertain themselves. At some time during the cruise, everyone finds his or her way to the Nautilus Room, which provides underwater viewing of the sea creatures accompanying the ship on its way. Two thick plates of glass and powerful lights provide the window to this mysterious undersea world. Special guest lecturers are scheduled (who and when varies) to make the cruise an educational experience.

This cruise line is notable, too, because of its no-tipping policy. The well-trained staff expect to make life comfortable for you as part of their service.

You may find the ports of call a little unfamiliar sometimes, because the Seabourn crew wants you to discover what is still unknown to the crowd. Of course, there will be stops at familiar ports, too, but the unexpected becomes the expected on a Seabourn cruise. Although you may never want to leave the comfort of the ship, the line offers many attractive land excursion packages to enhance your trip.

The Seabourn Spa is a complete fitness center in which to work out or relax with a massage or a body wrap. There are classes to attend, (or not, depending on your mood). In the showroom, you will enjoy music ranging from swing to jazz. You can be entertained or you can dance. Day or night, you will be surrounded by the quiet, refined ambience of an exclusive club.

Sun Line Cruises
1 Rockefeller Plaza, Suite 315
New York, NY 10020
(212) 397-6400
800-445-6400
$$–$$$

For exotic destinations, choose Sun Lines. Its Amazon cruises feature on-board lectures to make the experience rich and rewarding.

Learn about botany and ecology first-hand. If you decide to take the carnival in Rio cruise, the company will arrange for you to enjoy the activities in that city.

Sun Line also will take you on a grand European transatlantic cruise that includes eleven ports on three continents, with stops at Monte Carlo, Florence, and Rome and in the South Atlantic.

This is one of the luxury liners that helped build the Greek reputation for excellence on the seas. Each crew member on the all-Greek staff has been there for an average of more than 16 years. Service their only goal.

Caribbean and Mexican Cruises

A quick voyage into the leisurely world of cruising is available with the short-voyage packages available in the Caribbean. You can enjoy land and cruise packages designed to give you a variety of vacation experiences.

Admiral Cruises
1050 Caribbean Way
Miami, FL 33132
(305) 374-1611
800-327-0271
$-$$

Admiral caters to your special interests and

needs in a variety of ways. Its three-night and four-night trips in the Bahamas and seven-night Mexican cruises give you a choice of special entertainment cruises. Sail with your favorite performing artists and enjoy big band or country music, depending on the cruise, for listening, dancing, and reminiscing.

Admiral offers special menus, including kosher foods, vegetarian selections, and menu items prepared within the guidelines of the American Heart Association. The *Emerald Seas* provides a fully equipped handicapped cabin.

Admiral provides land and cruise packages that allow passengers to stretch their vacation experience and get a taste of the areas near the cruise destinations. These are value-priced cruises that provide a lot of activity and variety.

Admiral also sails to Alaska.

Bermuda Star Line
800 Douglas Road, Suite 600
Coral Gables, FL 33134
(305) 529-3000
800-237-5361
$–$$

Departing from New Orleans, the *Queen of Bermuda* sails the Gulf of Mexico and visits Key West, a historic town that seems to have stopped in time. Then it sails to Playa del Carmen, where passengers can visit Mayan ruins on land excursions, shop, or enjoy the beach. Finally it visits Cozumel for its fabulous nightlife. Combined with a weekend in New Orleans, it's a cross-cultural vacation filled with excitement and romance.

This is a classic ship, rich in the tradition of cruise vessels. The accommodations are spacious and the service attentive. Like most cruise ships, the accent is on great dining, almost around the clock.

This ship also sails the Mexican Riviera and takes fall cruises to catch the color up the coast to New England and Canada.

Carnival Cruise Lines
3655 NW 87th Avenue
Miami, FL 33178
(305) 599-2600
800-327-7373

Carnival has the "fun ships" with the reputation of nonstop fun and excitement. Affordable prices on three-, four-, and seven-day cruises have encouraged many first-time cruise travelers to join the fun. The atmosphere on these cruises is upbeat, activity-oriented, and youthful. You will mingle with the cocoa-butter crowd on these lively cruises.

Chandris Fantasy Cruises
900 Third Avenue
New York, NY 10022
800-437-3111
$

Chandris may catch your attention simply because of their kids-cruise-free policy. You can have two grandchildren sharing a cabin with two full-fare adults. Since Fantasy Tours also specializes in holiday cruises, this could help the family get together for an unforgettable vacation. If you're over 65, save 50 percent when sharing a room with a full-fare companion.

Chandris also has quick getaway trips, such as its Champagne Weekend cruises. Don't overlook the longer voyages when you have a week or two to spend at sea. With 20 cruise destinations, Chandris is a leader in Caribbean cruises. Its Sea and Stay land and cruise programs let you enjoy a bit of Florida with your cruise. These fun folks also stage murder mystery and wine-tasting cruises.

Chandris also sails in the Mediterranean and Europe.

Dolphin Cruise Line
1007 North America Way
Miami, FL 33132
(They prefer that you contact your travel agent.)

Dolphin can give you a little or a lot of the Caribbean. Choose a 3- or 4-night getaway or a 7- or 14-night vacation. Depending on your itinerary, you might explore San Juan or Nassau, Cozumel or Montego Bay. There are a lot of different cultures you will sample as you visit the various ports of call.

You can join one of the theme cruises, where you'll enjoy golden oldies, jazz, or classical music. You even can participate in the murder mystery cruises. Plan to bring your own costume for the masquerade party and your sheet music for talent night.

Premier Cruise Lines
400 Challenger Road
Cape Canaveral, FL 32920
(407) 783-5061
800-327-7113
$–$$

Premier is the official cruise line of Walt Disney World. That should tell you something about its commitment to family fun and good value. The cruise line is the largest in the three- and four-day Bahamas cruise market. With land and cruise packages that give you a little of the Caribbean as well as a taste of Disney World (or Epcot Center), you and other family members will have plenty to do.

On board, there are special programs to keep the kids occupied under the supervision of the professional counselors. First Mates is for the little ones from ages 2 to 4; Kids Call has activities for the 5 to 7 year olds; Starcruiser activities are designed for the 8 to 12 year olds; and Teen Cruiser activities are just for those aged 13 to 17. And who knows kids better than the Disney folks? The activity schedules give you some leisure time to spend with adult company.

At night, family-oriented entertainment, including comedy and music, is staged on board. To stay physically active, there's Sea-Sport, a program that includes dance, aerobics, team sports, and a health spa. There's a trademark "up" beat with a touch of summer camp enthusiasm to all of the activities. This generation-spanning vacation can liven up the spirits.

The Kid's Quarters™ concept lets you have a separate stateroom for children at a considerable savings so that you can have some privacy and a break from the kids for yourself. For more economy, or if you prefer the children stay with you, choose the large four- or five-berth staterooms.

Premier is perfectly suited for multigeneration vacations. The programs, amenities, and optional separate quarters let you provide a memorable vacation for both you and your grandchildren, without any nerve-racking strain.

Princess Cruises
(Contact your travel agent.)
$–$$
The famed "Love Boat" cruises the Caribbean regularly. For information about the cruise line, refer to the previous "Luxury Worldwide Cruises" section (pages 213-225).

Windstar Sail Cruises
300 Elliott Avenue West
Seattle, WA 98119
(Consult your travel agent.)
$$$
Sail the Caribbean, and also Tahiti, the Mediterranean, and Alaska, on one of the most exciting ships at sea. An elite group of 148 passengers can enjoy a cruise on *Wind Song*, a 440-foot sailing vessel. With its exquisite interiors and gourmet dining, this ship has the ambience of a private yacht.

Something Special Cruises

Cruise lines, anxious to attract passengers, have elevated theme cruises to a fine art. There are singles cruises, fitness cruises, seminars at sea, and many other interest-oriented voyages to make sure you find compatible companions to share your adventure.

The trips highlighted just hint at the rich experiences open to you. Cruise consultants and the cruise lines themselves will tell you what current adventures are available. The common denominator is that you will meet active people your own age who share your interests. Those cruises that specialize in the bikini beat have been passed over in favor of the glorious cruises designed for travelers looking for something more to do than baste themselves in coconut oil suntan lotion.

DANCE CRUISES

Merry Widows Dance Cruises
PO Box 31087
Tampa, FL 33622
(Contact your AAA travel agent.)

Here's an exciting option for single women (whether unmarried, divorced, or widowed) that offers you an opportunity to kick up your heels in a safe, nonpressured environment.

Four times a year, the Merry Widows Dance Cruises take women who love to dance, but who have no dance partner, on cruises where they can dance night after night.

Dance hosts ranging in age from 35 to 65 are selected from professional dance studios across the country. Their expenses are paid by the participants, but they receive no salary or tips. There are always enough partners that you can enjoy many dances on your cruise. In fact, your dance cards are designed to give you an opportunity to dance with each partner before the end of the cruise. You will dine with these charming gentlemen as well; they rotate nightly from table to table to provide lively conversation for their companions.

This program has organized memorable cruises for many years, and the satisfied repeat passengers attest to success of the concept. The way the cruises are structured gives you complete freedom to enjoy yourself without any of the pressure or embarrassment you might experience on a regular cruise.

NATURALIST CRUISES

There's a new breed of cruises that are part of the burgeoning educational trend in travel. Passengers, bored with the prospect of another trip jammed with nonstop fun and frivolity, have graduated to these cruises. Noted scholars explain the natural history along the way. One plus is that these cruises tend to be on smaller, more intimate ships, with the kinds of amenities that are attractive to the experienced traveler (larger staterooms, a cozier environment).

Clipper Cruise Line
7711 Bonhomme
St. Louis, MO 63105
(314) 727-2929
800-325-0010
$$
Typifying the new naturalist cruise trend is the Clipper Cruise Line. This snappy three-ship company is specifically targeting the more mature (that is, experienced) traveler who prefers a deeper look at natural history along the way and visits to less-familiar destinations. The largest of its ships carries fewer than 150 passengers, assuring a companionable voyage with like-minded individuals. The ship has naturalists on board to lecture. You are sure to return from your trip with a greater understanding and appreciation of nature and its surroundings.

Society Expeditions Cruises
3131 Elliott Avenue, Suite 700
Seattle, WA 98121
(206) 285-9400
800-426-7794
$$–$$$

Preview the cruises on videotapes, which may be in the library of your cruise consultant, to whet your appetite for truly exotic voyages. If you can't find them, they are available from the company for a modest price (under $10). These fabulous videos bring spectacular views of the scenery plus delightful scenes with native wildlife. There are *Project Amazon, South Pacific and Indonesia,* as well as *Project Antarctica and Subantarctica.* As the name of the cruise line implies, these are serious cruises for travelers intent on learning and sharing their concern for the last wild frontiers on earth.

World Explorer Cruises
555 Montgomery Street
San Francisco, CA 94111
(415) 391-9262
800-854-3835
$–$$

This company skillfully combines an interesting cruise itinerary with land excursion packages to provide an in-depth exploration of Alaska. By most definitions, this is not a luxury cruise. Yet the accommodations are comfortable and the on-board atmosphere is relaxed and casual.

Every cruise has a shipboard faculty of three or four experts on Alaska. There's a 12,000–book library filled with works devoted to Alaska. This educational trip is so serious that you actually can receive extension credits through California's Chapman College.

With more than forty shore excursions, you can explore Alaska's interior by float plane, raft, canoe, or rail.

Your evenings on the ship will be filled with slide shows, lectures, and movies. The ambience of the ship is mirrored in the ever-present classical music, which provides a regal sound-track for the beauty you will be observing.

Their mission is to give you a glimpse of the "real" Alaska, glitz- and glamour-free. They strive to provide "a 14-day adventure for the mind, heart and soul."

Holland America Line
Westours Inc.
300 Elliott Avenue West
Seattle, WA 98119
(206) 281-3535
800-426-0327
(Consult your travel agent.)
$–$$

The appeal of this cruise to Alaska is that you will travel on a luxury ship and the land tours are fully escorted. Perhaps a bit less scholarly in approach than some others, it is nonetheless a fascinating and educational look at the "last frontier." You will see Alaska from a variety of vantage points, and all along the way you will have stories and folklore described by seasoned guides. The driver-guides undergo an intensive sixteen-week certification course, and tour directors must complete a two and a half–week course on culture, art, history, and wildlife.

The inland portions of your trip will be via Westours' own motorcoaches and private glass-domed rail cars. You also will enjoy day-light tours of inland waterways via Westours' excursion boats and accommodations in its hotels. This is what the industry calls "integrated tourism," which means that every step of your journey is handled by the company's own people and using its own facilities. This can take some uncertainty out of the trip and assure you of consistent quality throughout your journey.

Crystal Cruises
2121 Avenue of the Stars
Los Angeles, CA 90067
(213) 785-9300
(Consult your travel agent.)
$$–$$$

If you want the glory of Alaska and absolutely world-class accommodations, Crystal Cruises may be your choice. The Alaska–Canada cruises let you soak up the culture and the lore, but from the comfort of the unparalleled luxury ship. You can certainly observe the wildlife and majestic beauty of the rugged terrain. This ship provides one of the most extensive lecture series programs in the industry, but it may cover a vast array of subjects beyond Alaskan natural history.

To keep fit at sea, Crystal offers an aquaerobics class and a spa, or you can jog around the deck.

You will revel in the creature comforts provided. Staterooms have space to spare, including a sitting area and a full-size tub. Fluffy goose down pillows and in-room VCRs are the kinds of touches that let you know that every detail has been handled with grace and style.

This cruise line has been in operation for over 100 years. It knows what it takes to keep passengers happy: food, service, and lovely accommodations.

If you are a naturalist, you also will want to contact Sun Line Cruises for their Amazon lecture cruise (see pages 224-225). For an adventure to the Galápagos, contact Galápagos Cruises/Adventure Associates (page 257).

WHALE-WATCHING EXCURSIONS

Up and down California's coast, there are ample opportunities to take day trips on ships that will take you out to see the whales. The gray whales, once near extinction, now migrate south every winter, and they come close to shore.

In spring the migration returns northward. You can see from one to a dozen whales surface and spout water. Although there are site stations on land, the best view is from the boats operated by nonprofit groups or sports fishing charters. These minicruise excursions easily can be slipped into the busiest travel schedule when you are visiting the coast. Costs vary.

In San Francisco:

Ocean Alliance
Fort Mason Center, Building E
San Francisco, CA 94123
(415) 441-5970

Captain John's
Pillar Point Harbor
Princeton by the Sea
PO Box 155
Half Moon Bay, CA 94019
(415) 728-3377
(415) 726-2913

In Monterey:

Sam's Fishing Fleet
84 Fisherman's Wharf
Monterey, CA 93940
(408) 372-0577

In Orange County:

Orange County Marine Institute
24200 Dana Point Harbor Drive
Dana Point, CA 92629
(714) 831-3850

The institute offers group tours only. Call ahead for reservations and pricing information.

In Los Angeles: *Mailing address:*

Catalina Channel
   Express   PO Box 1391
Berth 95   San Pedro, CA 90733
San Pedro, CA 90731 (213) 519-7971

Catalina Cruises
(213) 514-3838
   Computerized telephone information will give you directions to various departure points, schedules, and prices.

Spirit Sailing Cruises
Berth 75
San Pedro, CA 90731
(213) 831-1073

In San Diego:

Baja Expeditions
2625 Garnet Avenue
San Diego, CA 92109
(619) 581-3311

San Diego Natural History Museum
1788 El Pedro
San Diego, CA 92109

Mailing address:

PO Box 1390
San Diego, CA 92112
(619) 232-3821

CRUISES FOR MUSIC LOVERS

Commodore Cruise Line
800 Douglas Road, Suite 660
Coral Gables, FL 33134
800-237-5361
$

This creative cruise line offers many theme cruises, from its popular Remember When cruises, with your favorite performers of the fifties and sixties, to a Country-Western Cruise and a popular Oktoberfest, which feature the music and food to create just the right mood for the cruise theme. This line also offers a popular Arts and Crafts Cruise, which provides training in craft skills.

The "happy ship", as Commodore bills itself, stages a party every night as it sails the Caribbean. Whatever the cruise theme, during the day there's always the sun and expansive Caribbean beaches at the ports of call, plus water sports, shopping, and the kind of great dining you'd expect from an island cruise.

Epirotiki Lines
551 Fifth Avenue
New York, NY 10176
800-221-2470
$$–$$$

If music is your love, take the Music Festival Cruise, which will take you to Venice, Corfu, Genoa, and other ports while providing enriching concerts with world-acclaimed artists on board or in theaters at port cities. This adventure will give you the opportunity to meet the musicians and participate in discussions with critics and musicologists. Even during the day you will find musicians playing on the decks or in the lounges. Staged by the Cruise World Society, these cruises have gained in popularity since they were first launched in 1988.

The accommodations are first class, as you would expect from a cruise designed to attract the discriminating traveler. Yet the cost is not out of line, considering the depth of the cruise experience available.

They also offer a Holy Land cruise and an astrology cruise. Note also that this cruise line offers a kosher menu.

Music theme trips also are available with Delta Queen (next page) and Admiral Cruises (page 225).

RIVER CRUISES

Delta Queen Steamboat Company
No. 30 Robin Street Wharf
New Orleans, LA 70130
(504) 586-0631
800-543-7637
$-$$$

These are the last of the overnight paddle wheelers. It seems that steamboating delights just about any age, so multigeneration family trips are popular. When you're sailing up the Mississippi, relaxing on a deck rocker, it's easy to be transported back in time to when steamboats were the lifeline of the riverside communities. By observing the world at a different pace, suddenly you have time for real conversation with friends or family.

Delta Queen plans special cruises, including big band vacations and the fifties "Rock Around the Clock" vacation. Your days and nights will be filled with the music you love for dancing and romancing. You can enjoy a Southern Celebrations Cruise when the azaleas and magnolias bloom. Enjoy fall foliage cruises, holiday cruises (great for families), or a Wilderness Rivers voyage. You can schedule a New Orleans expedition to explore the river and the city. Or perhaps best yet, there's the Odyssey, which takes you the full length of the Mississippi, or trips on both the Ohio and Mississippi rivers.

Every meal aboard the steamboats has at least one selection in keeping with the dietary guidelines of the American Heart Association. There are limited facilities for handicapped passengers; check on the details before making your reservation.

Choose a 2-night getaway or a 14-night vacation on this legendary steamboat line. No other experience can match it.

KD German Rhine Line
170 Hamilton Avenue
White Plains, NY 10601-1788
(914) 948-3600
800-346-6525 (east of the Mississippi River)
and
323 Geary Street, Suite 603
San Francisco, CA 94102-1860
(415) 392-8817
800-858-8587
$–$$$

The Three-River Cruise will take you past vineyards and towns along the Rhine and its tributaries. Four- or six-day cruises provide leisurely sightseeing from the vessel and many sightseeing opportunities in Cologne, Strasborg, and other cities along the route. Choose the Grand Europe Cruise, the Castles and Wine Cruise, or the Floating Wine Seminar. Your cabin is a sitting room by day, a bedroom at night. All accommodations, regardless of size, are outside rooms with a view.

BARGING

Technically, barging could be considered a riverboat cruise. However, it is such a unique travel experience, it must be in a class by itself. Barging, as defined by the Europeans, is one of the most elegant ways to travel. On a deluxe yachtlike vessel, you and a small group (sometimes as few as a dozen) drift down picturesque waterways at a hare's pace of approximately three miles per hour. This actually gives you the chance to hop off the boat on a given day (particularly if the vessel has to spend some time negotiating through locks) and sightsee. Then, catch up with your boat and reboard in time for dinner.

Each trip is as unique as the barge you travel on and the canal system you traverse. Your vantage point always will give you a unique perspective on the countryside or cities you see.

You may want to try your first barge trip with the only American company selling barge trips in France:

French Country Waterways
PO Box 2195
Duxbury, MA 02331
(617) 934-2454 (in Massachusetts)
800-222-1236
$$$

Another company that has a loyal following in this specialized field is:

Floating Through Europe
271 Madison Avenue
New York, NY 10016
(212) 685-5600 (in New York City)
800-221-3140
$$–$$$

Also ask your travel agent for tour details from two other barge specialists. They can assure you delightful voyages in England, Germany, France, or Turkey:

Abercrombie & Kent
1520 Kensington Road, Suite 212
Oak Brook, IL 60521
(708) 954-2944 (in Illinois)
800-323-7308
$$$

Joli Tours
19 West 34th Street, Suite 1219
New York, NY 10001
(212) 695-5654
800-333-JOLI
$$$

SPAS AT SEA

There is hardly a cruise ship today that does not have some sort of spa or recreation program supervised by the social director. Typically you'll find a whirlpool and frequently a masseuse. But some cruise lines have gotten more serious about pursuing the fitness buff and the individual who wants a spa-at-sea experience.

Cunard Line
555 Fifth Avenue
New York, NY 10017
800-221-4770 (Cunard reservations)
800-458-9000 (Sea Goddess reservations)
Cunard has launched the exclusive Golden Door Spa at Sea, which echoes the luxury and pampering of its namesake. Available only on Cunard's luxury vessels, the spa provides daily fitness schedules supervised by professionals as well as personal services to relax away the tension. In addition, there is consultation

available for stress management, nutrition, and weight training.

When sailing on the Sea Goddess vessels, you will enjoy the intimate yachtlike ambience of a small ship. The company will even send you a personal preference list prior to sailing to inquire about your particular tastes in food and beverages. This, combined with the spa cuisine, will ensure that you enjoy every tasty morsel during your cruise.

Costa Cruises
World Trade Center
80 SW 8th Street
Miami, FL 33130-3097
(305) 358-7325
800-462-6782
$–$$$

This is luxury Italian-style! You can enjoy a complete range of pampering routines as well as utilize a fully outfitted gym in the SpaCosta program. While sailing through the Caribbean, Alaska, the Mediterranean, or the Far East, you will have professionals to tend to your health, fitness, and beauty. The menus have the gourmet spa selections you would expect on a luxury liner.

FREIGHTERS

When you have more time to spend and a powerful sense of adventure, traveling the world on a freighter can be an exciting course in world culture. Usually there are fewer than a dozen passengers on board. You eat with the crew, and while the food is good and plentiful, it isn't the nonstop parade of cuisine offered by the cruise ships — a welcome change for many passengers. Your accommodations will be comfortable, however, not luxurious. These cruises average about $100 per day or less, depending on the cruise.

Your stays in the various ports of call may last a day or two or longer as cargo is loaded or unloaded. Days are unstructured and casual, with no need for elaborate wardrobe changes. Some boats are installing pools, really the only amenity some people have missed. The accommodations are comfortable and normally have private baths.

Some companies specialize in this type of travel. Be forewarned that with fewer than 12 passengers aboard, there won't be a ship's doctor. Your doctor may have to vouch in writing for your health and fitness.

Cruise and Freighter Association
PO Box 188
Flushing, NY 11358
(718) 939-2400
800-548-7823 (in Canada)
800-872-8584
$

For $15 a year or $25 for two years, you can get a copy of *TravLtips,* which will give you the inside story on freighter travel. It is written by subscribers themselves. This organization also will act as your travel agent to book you on the freighter cruise of your choice.

Freighter World Cruises
180 South Lake Avenue, Suite 335
Pasadena, CA 91101
(818) 449-3106
$

When a company specializes in one facet of travel, such as freighter cruises, you know they have the experience to guide a novice. They can advise you on various cruises available and give you information about what to expect on this kind of adventure.

Cruise Discounts

With the advent of the three- and four-day

cruises, you no longer have to have an extended block of time or unlimited funds to enjoy a cruise. In fact, even the longer cruises are available at a discount if you know how to shop.

It isn't difficult for passengers, regardless of age, to find discounted rates. The cruise lines currently are overbuilt and set sail with empty berths regularly. To entice you, cruise lines have a variety of money-saving tactics. One you will encounter quickly is the early book–early pay incentive. If you can book months in advance, you can get substantial discounts or a number of add-on benefits, such as free land packages, to enhance your trip.

The flip side of that logic is that also those who are able to pick up and leave on a moment's notice can enjoy substantial discounts. In addition to the information available through the cruise consultants already mentioned, talk to the last-minute cruise discounters.

Spur of the Moment Cruises
10780 Jefferson Boulevard
Culver City, CA 90230
(213) 838-9329 (24-hour recorded information)
(213) 839-2418
800-343-1991

This is a clearinghouse for last-minute unsold cabins. The company buys up inventory at drastic reductions and offers it to the public at 25 to 65 percent off retail rates. You can get on their mailing list free or call anytime day or night for recorded information.

If you feel gutsy and are willing to walk away if the deal isn't right, choose a ship that is ready to leave dock, approach the crew member in charge of passenger embarkation, and negotiate a favorable deal. After all, once the ship leaves port, there is no value to an empty cabin.

That same logic means that single passengers who want private accommodations probably can negotiate, or have their travel agent arrange, for the single supplement charge to be waived. As long as they are not losing revenue because you are traveling alone, your negotiating position is strong.

You can look for discounts of up to 50 percent or more on cruises booked for the off-seasons, when fewer people travel. Often these can be the most charming trips because the pressure is off the crew, and with fewer passengers, the companionship between shipmates is more cordial.

Age-specific discounts are not as prevalent here as in other parts of the travel industry;

however, follow the rule of thumb, and ask. Like airline seats, discounts may be available at one time and not at another, depending on occupancy. Nevertheless, Premier Cruises plus a number of highly competitive Caribbean cruise lines have been known to offer discounts. In addition, AARP, other 50+ clubs, travel agents specializing in the 50+ market, and various travel clubs can negotiate better rates than you might find for yourself.

But here's something you should know: many experienced cruise passengers feel that price is not always the object. Since cruises are an investment, most people would rather make sure they have the right cruise than a cruise whose only advantage is price.

Cruise Hotlines

This extensive list of worldwide cruise lines and cruise consultants, compiled with the help of industry insiders, includes many companies not mentioned previously. This does not imply that any are less worthy. It does mean you will have to determine whether or not the cruises they offer are suitable for your lifestyle and budget. These numbers are provided as a convenience as you research cruises. If one sounds interesting, your cruise consultant or travel agent may be your best resource for information. In fact, the advice previously given still holds true: trust a qualified travel agent, one with Cruise Lines International Association membership to insure cruise expertise.

Please note that most cruise companies prefer to deal with travel professionals only. Try your own travel agent or one of the cruise consultants first; call the company only if you are unable to secure information any other way.

As mentioned at the beginning of the cruise section, you can secure a list of cruise-only agents by sending a self-addressed, stamped envelope to:

National Association of Cruise Only Agents
PO Box 7209
Freeport, NY 11520

CONSULTANTS AND CRUISE PLANNERS (TRAVEL AGENTS OR CRUISE WHOLESALERS)

Abercrombie & Kent/
  Continental Waterways
(708) 954-2944 (in Illinois)
800-323-7308

Barge About France — Quiz Tour
(209) 733-7119
800-323-7436

Canberra Cruises
(212) 629-3630 (in New York)
800-223-5799

Club Mediterranee
800-258-2633

Cruise Company
(203) 622-0203 (in Connecticut)
800-825-0826

Cruise & Freighter Association
(718) 939-2400
800-548-7823 (in Canada)
800-872-8584

Cruises of Distinction
(201) 744-1331 (in New Jersey)
800-634-3445

Dirigo Cruises
(203) 669-7068 (in Connecticut)
800-845-5520

Esplanade Tours
Art Treasures and Natural History Cruises
800-628-4893 (in Massachusetts)
800-426-5492

Floating Through Europe Barge Trips
(212) 685-5600 (in New York)
800-221-3140

Freighter World Cruises
(818) 449-3106

Galapágos Cruises/Adventure Associates
(214) 907-0414 (in Texas)
800-527-2500

Hapag-Lloyd Tours
(516) 794-1253 (in New York)
800-334-2724

Hilton Nile Cruises
800-445-8667

International Cruise Center
Represents Soviet Passenger Ships;
  River Cruises
(516) 747-8880 (in New York)
800-221-3254

Landry and Kling
(305) 661-1880 (in Florida)
800-448-9002 (in California)
800-431-4007

Merry Widows Dance Cruises
(Through AAA or your travel agent)

Raymond and Whitcomb
(212) 759-3960

Regency Cruises
(212) 972-4499

South Florida Cruises
(305) 739-SHIP
800-327-SHIP

Spur of the Moment Cruises
(213) 838-9329 (twenty-four-hour recorded
    information)
(213) 839-2418
800-233-2129 (in California, but not in the
    213, 818, or 714 area codes)
800-343-1991

CRUISE LINES

Admiral Cruises
(305) 374-1611
800-327-0271

American Canadian Caribbean Line
(401) 247-0955 (in Rhode Island)
800-556-7450

Bergen Line
(212) 986-2711 (in New York)
800-323-7436

Bermuda Star Line
(201) 837-0400
800-237-5361

Carnival Cruise Lines
(305) 599-2600
800-327-7373

Chandris Celebrity and
  Chandris Fantasy Cruises
(212) 750-0044 (in New York)
800-437-3111

Classical Cruises
(212) 794-3200
800-252-7745

Clipper Cruise Line
(314) 727-2929 (in Missouri)
800-325-0010

Commodore Cruise Line
800-237-5361

Costa Cruises
(305) 358-7325
800-462-6782

Crown Cruise Line
(407) 845-7447 (in Florida)
800-841-7447

Crystal Cruises
(213) 785-9300
Book through your travel agent

Cunard Line
800-221-4770

Delta Queen Steamboat Line
(504) 586-0631
800-543-7637

Dolphin Cruise Line
Book through your travel agent

Dolphin Hellas Cruises
(213) 544-3551

Epirotiki Lines
800-221-2470

French Country Waterways
Barge Tours
(617) 934-2454 (in Massachusetts)
800-222-1236

French Cruise Lines
800-222-8664

Holland America Line
(206) 281-3535
800-426-0327
Book through your travel agent

Ivaran Lines
(212) 809-1220 (in New York)
800-451-1639

KD German Rhine Line
(914) 948-3600 (in New York)
800-346-6525 (east of the Mississippi
    River)
800-858-8587 (west of the Mississippi
    River)

Mediterranean Shipping Company
(212) 691-3760
800-666-9333

Norwegian Cruise Line
(305) 447-9660
800-327-7030

Ocean Cruise Line/Pearl Cruises
(305) 764-3500 (in Florida)
800-426-3588

Ocean Quest International
(504) 586-8686
800-338-3483

Oceanic Cruises
(415) 227-0781
800-545-5778

Paquet French Cruises
(407) 659-3460 (in Florida)
800-999-0555

Premier Cruise Lines
(407) 783-5061
800-327-7113

Princess Cruises
Book through your travel agent

Renaissance Cruises
(305) 463-0982
800-525-2450

Royal Caribbean Cruise Lines
(305) 379-2601
800-327-6700

Royal Cruise Line
(415) 956-7200 (information)
(415) 788-0610 (reservations)

Royal Viking Line
(305) 447-9660
800-422-8000

St. Lawrence Cruise Lines
(613) 549-8091
800-267-7868

Seabourn Cruise Line
(415) 391-7444 (information)
800-351-9595 (reservations)

Society Expeditions Cruises
(206) 285-9400 (in Washington)
800-426-7794

Sun Line Cruises
(212) 397-6400 (in New York)
800-445-6400
800-368-3888 (in Canada)

Swan Hellenic and Swan
  Hellenic Nile Cruises
(617) 266-7465
800-426-5492

Tall Ship Adventures
(303) 341-0335
800-662-0090

Viking Yacht Cruises of Greece
(203) 226-7911
800-341-3030

Windjammer Barefoot Cruises
(305) 672-6453
800-432-3364 (in Florida)
800-327-2601
800-233-2603 (in Canada)

Windstar Sail Cruises
(See Holland America Line)

World Explorer Cruises
(415) 391-9262
800-854-3835

Trains

There are those who contend that when traveling by rail, getting there is just as exciting as being there. And with the rail cars that have been restored to their original opulence, reflecting the glory days of travel by rail, train travel takes on a sense of time travel as well.

The Europeans never lost rail travel as a primary means of transportation, yet somehow Americans, enamored with high-speed jets, almost let the industry disappear. Fortunately for romantics, rail travel is enjoying a comeback in this country. Here are some hand-picked train adventures in the U.S., Canada, and abroad.

There are two main categories of rail trips available to you. One is actual point-to-point transportation via rail (sometimes in exquisite accommodations). The other is the jaunt or tour that takes you to or through a scenic area for a few hours, providing nostalgic glimpses of the legendary train travel of the past.

Now that you have the leisure to travel at a smell-the-roses pace, maybe the roses should be the fresh ones in the dining car or in a country garden you may discover on a stop along the way. Best of all, you have an appreciation for the qualities that made train travel so popular in the first place — service, scenery, and social life.

Omni Senior Rail Tours
1 Northfield Plaza
Northfield, IL 60093
(Consult your travel agent)

   If rail travel appeals to you but you are hesitant to plan your own trip, here is a tour company catering to the 50+ traveler. Omni combines rail, motorcoach, and even air travel when necessary, to create one-of-a-kind trips to favored destinations. You can visit Florida, Texas, the old South, and the West Coast, among other regions. Take in spring blooms or fall foliage by scheduling your tours by the calendar.

Point-to-Point Rail Travel

American-European Express
River Place, Suite 402
329 West Eighteenth Street
Chicago, IL 60616
(312) 226-5558
800-677-4233

   For all-out elegance, nothing compares with the American-European Express Railway Train Deluxe, which provides nightly service between Chicago and Washington, D.C. The train is operated in association with the Nostalgie Istanbul Orient Express, the last word in luxury train travel.

Each train has three sleepers, a dining car, and a club car. The special caravan of cars is attached to the regularly scheduled Aıntrak train that travels between the two cities.

All sleeping compartments have a private water closet and sink, individually controlled heat and air-conditioning, and luggage storage. Sleeping cars, each with a shower compartment, offer a choice of accommodations: car bedrooms for two, or drawing rooms, which sleep two or three. For a truly luxurious train experience, there is the Presidential Cabin, which has more space and a private shower.

The dining car, richly decorated with Honduran mahogany and accented with original art, serves meals on fine china and linens. The evening seven-course meal is a unique event for today's traveler. There is also a club car with a full-service bar and live piano music.

To insure the highest level of service, the passenger list is restricted to 56 and is served by a staff of 13. Although the accommodations are eagerly sought by harried, plane-weary business executives who desire some uninterrupted meetings en route to Washington or back, the leisure traveler is likely to get hooked on the superior service and sumptuous surroundings as well. This is a change of pace that rekindles one's spirit of adventure in train travel.

Venice Simplon-Orient Express
1155 Avenue of the Americas 30th Floor
New York, NY 10036
(212) 302-5055
800-524-2420

Experience what royalty and celebrities have enjoyed since the heyday of grand train travel. This is the grandeur of the twenties and thirties. Operating for more than a century now, this train, which, candidly, had lost some of its grace, has been lovingly restored to its original splendor, a time machine to take you across Europe and back in time.

Visit all of the cities you love: Venice, Vienna, Monte Carlo, Paris, and Zurich. Combine your train adventure with a glorious cruise on the Orient Express and add exotic ports of call to your itinerary. There are also Orient Express Hotels strategically placed worldwide. If you can't make the cross-continental trip, opt for a day excursion on the British Pullman in southern England.

This is living history. The carriages are splendidly decorated with inlaid woods, fabric panels, etched glass, and rich lacquers. This is Old World craftsmanship so refined, it's like traveling in a museum (without an ounce of stuffiness).

Need it be mentioned that the cuisine is excellent? Finish an evening over cognac in the bar car while being entertained by the pianist. Whereas other European trains would invite denim and deck shoes, the Orient-Express invites passengers to participate with a sense of occasion. The kind of casual elegance you would expect on a yacht or at the country club would be appropriate. In the evening, black tie is encouraged for gentlemen, while women wear gowns reminiscent of the twenties or at least cocktail finery.

If this all sounds like too much effort (or snobbery) to you, this isn't the train experience you're looking for. But if it sounds like the most fun you could have on a rail adventure, it could be the highlight of your traveling career. You really have to be willing to get into the swing of it, or frankly, it won't be worth it. Expect to meet some imaginative time travelers who want to recreate a lost era, if only for a moment.

Abercrombie & Kent International
1520 Kensington Road, Suite 212
Oak Brook, IL 60521
(708) 954-2944 (in Illinois)
800-323-7308

These imaginative people design train trips that you might have thought existed only in your fantasies. You can choose any one of the trips for an experience that even the most savvy traveler can find deeply satisfying. These are tours that are particularly appealing to the most-experienced, independent individuals. You will travel by Europe's finest trains, in first-class comfort. At night, you might be as likely to stay in a quaint local inn as an elegant hotel, but rest assured, the standards of quality are consistently high, whatever adventure is planned for you.

Yes, you will have a guide to fill you in on the rich local history and cultural aspects of your trip, but you will retain a refreshing measure of independence so that you can explore on your own and have the distinct pleasure of personal discovery. These trips, centered around train travel, are designed to let you visit some less-traveled, but no-less-interesting, territory.

Choose the Great Britain and Europe Express for an in-depth view of England,

Wales, France, Italy, Switzerland, Spain, and Germany. There's no other way to take in the scenery with quite the abandon that is yours aboard Europe's first-class trains.

Delve deeply into the beauty and culture of Scotland on the Royal Scotsman Tour. You will find out why experienced travelers rave about the Scottish railways. Your all-inclusive rate will cover meals, hotels, and transportation along the way. You will even have the opportunity to visit some private castles not open to the general public with your intimate group (thirty-two maximum). You'll love the observation car, previously a salon for the chief general manager of the London and North Eastern Railway.

On the Anna Karenina, you will discover the countryside of Russia in a way seldom seen by Westerners. These are the only private railway carriages in all of Russia. These cars provide self-sufficient travel accommodations for a small group of travelers and are able to withstand the weather extremes with heat and air-conditioning. Your meals are included, prepared from fresh ingredients brought on the train daily. When you do have an opportunity to stay in Leningrad and Moscow, it is in Russia's finest hotels: the Astoria and Metropole.

Many jaded travelers have renewed their

enthusiasm for globe-trotting by finding the kinds of distinctive, private travel experience that you can enjoy with the exclusive Abercrombie and Kent tours. New people, new territory, and a new perspective can be yours, thanks to these exceptional train tours.

Amtrak
800-USA-RAIL

Today Amtrak has rail service across the country, with many package tours that let you take in the sights along the way. There is a variety of accommodations, from economy bedrooms, deluxe bedrooms, and family bedrooms, to slumbercoaches and roomettes. In addition, there are lounges, dining cars, buffet cars, and dinettes or cafés, depending on the length of your train trip. You can even take your car when you're heading to Florida.

Amtrak is bringing train travel back into vogue with a larger traveling public. The accommodations are comfortable, and the scenery enjoyed from the sightseer lounges is simply unforgettable. Amtrak tours include your hotel and often some meals. Reading the encyclopedic schedule, however, is a challenge. Your best bet is to call Amtrak or your travel agent to make sure you understand the details. Amtrak does try to accommodate handicapped passengers and those with special diets.

Alaska Railroad Corporation
PO Box 107500
Anchorage, AK 99510-7500
800-544-0552

You can see Alaska from a variety of vantage points as you take one of the tours planned by this railroad company. Rail-boat-bus tours or air-rail trips are available. You will visit such communities as Seward, a town of 2,200 surrounded by mountains and fjords. On one tour, there's even a sternwheeler riverboat cruise.

Blyth and Company
1 Rockefeller Plaza, Suite 1712
New York, NY 10020
(212) 265-9600

This tour operator has designed Canada's only transcontinental train service, spanning the distance between Vancouver and Toronto. The luxury 8-car train, with a maximum passenger load of just 188, operates along the Canadian Pacific Rail track.

As the Canadian wholesaler of the Orient-Express service, these people are deeply experienced in luxury train travel. With five bedroom cars, a lounge car, a dining car, and a utility car, this self-contained world is the picture of luxury. Every room has a private bath, phone, TV, and VCR.

The train offers 10 extraordinary accommodations, large staterooms with a private observation dome. Other accommodations are available, too, including connecting bedrooms that open into suites during the day, making this train a popular choice among traveling businesspeople. Add to that fax and telex capability and you might imagine this is a luxury office on rails. Fortunately, the vacationing passenger is well cared for, too, with superior service and outstanding cuisine. You can even order your special vegetarian, low-cal, or kosher food in advance.

The journey across Canada always has captured the imagination of seasoned travelers. Now it captures the heart as well, with unprecedented accommodations and service unavailable elsewhere in the country.

VIA
800-268-9503 (in Canada)
(In the United States, contact your
    travel agent)

VIA is the public train service for all of Canada. You can travel cross-country with a choice of coach, dayniter, or VIA 1 First Class service. VIA provides on-board meal service and domed lounges to enjoy the scenery. If time is limited, take the spectacular two-day Rocky Mountaineer trip, which features a stay in historic Kamloops, British Columbia.

Specialized Train Tours

The romance and luxury of train travel are not reserved for those with extensive vacation time and luxury budgets. There are a number of train trips that can give you the same experience by taking you on a journey for a few hours or days in restored historic or beautifully contemporary rail cars. The ambience, the food, the scenery, and the cordial companionship of fellow travelers are the same.

Augusta's Trolley Tour
1301 32 Eighth, Suite 200
PO Box 1331
Augusta, GA 30903-1331
(404) 823-6600
Buy an all-day ticket or pay 50¢ every time you board the Olde Town Trolley, which tours six historic districts of Augusta. Soak up the atmosphere that makes this city such a delight for history buffs. Plan to shop for antiques as well.

Conch Tour Train
601 Duval St., Suite 8
Key West, FL 33040
(305) 294-5161

Old Town Trolley
Key West, FL 33040
(305) 266-6688

Travel 14 miles and 400 years through historic Key West on the Conch Tour Train. You will see incredible natural beauty, the harbor, and traces of the days when pirates and Spanish conquistadors claimed Key West for themselves.

A one and a half-hour trolley tour is guided by congenial hosts who will let you in on the intriguing history of this tiny gulf community.

Napa Valley Wine Train
1275 McKinstry Street
Napa, CA 94559
(707) 253-2160

This luxury train combines the elegance of old-time train travel and the serene appeal of the beautiful wine country. With interiors based on the industry legend, the Orient Express, passengers can relax for several hours, drink in the gorgeous scenery, and enjoy a gourmet meal (brunch, lunch, or dinner). The train's service and atmosphere are clearly from the golden era of trains; the cuisine is distinctly elegant California cuisine. When you have just a few hours to jump back in time, this is the tour to take out of San Francisco.

Great Smoky Mountains Railway
1 Maple Street
Sylva, NC 28779
(704) 586-8811
800-872-4681

Here's a wonderful way to travel through North Carolina's "mountain vacationland." Seven counties are connected by rail to take you through natural wonderlands. Soak up some history and sample the culture. Day trips and special excursions take the guesswork out of travel planning.

Ontario Northland
65 Front Street West
Toronto, Ontario, Canada M5J 1E6
(416) 965-4268

The Polar Bear Express is a train that will take you through northern Ontario, a wilderness accessible only by rail or plane. Your four-hour trip will start at Cochrane and end at Moosonee, gateway to the Arctic, and Moose Factory Island, Ontario's oldest settlement. You will enjoy the scenery as you are served a hearty breakfast and mid-morning coffee en route.

Lamoille Valley Railroad
Stafford Avenue
Morrisville, VT 05661
(802) 888-4255

The train cars of yesteryear will take you through scenic mountains, crossing over one of the last covered bridges for trains in the country. A lucky 200 passengers make their way, as they have since the 1870s, past towns and farms, and rivers and meadows. This makes a never-to-be-forgotten tour of fall foliage and is definitely a place to bring extra film to play tourist. Pack the extra lenses for the photos you won't get anywhere else. The trip takes about two hours and covers about 40 miles of Vermont countryside. Make reservations to assure a space.

Trains Unlimited Tours
PO Box 1997
Portola, CA 96122
(916) 836-1745

A train buff named Chris Skow is responsible for this popular train tour company. Skow and fellow adventurers have taken trips through Central and South America via rail.

For a wider audience, Skow has developed a luxury train car, the Virginia City, which is coupled with scheduled trains, to emulate the luxurious travel of the wealthy. The train car travels primarily western routes, such as Oakland to Reno, often on special charters. However, tours also are scheduled for the public, including trips to Alaska. As the concept catches fire, more tours undoubtedly will be planned.

For other train tours, consult the "Motorcoach Tours" and "Cruises" sections (pages 283-290 and 207-264, respectively) and the chapter on guided tours (starting on page 306). You will find such companies as Mayflower Tours, Tours of Distinction, and the Holland America Line's Westours, which, among their many planned trips, include some via train. Grand Circle Travel, for example, can put you on the glorious Princess's "Midnight Sun Express."

Discounts

Like many discounts that are age-specific, various rail packages and passes may change without notice. Also, as you would with other travel and hospitality suppliers, you will want to inquire about the current low fares, even if they are not age-related. Some of these bargains, available to travelers of any age, are listed here. Generally you can rely on your travel agent to have current information on hand. Or call the sources listed for up-to-the-minute rates.

Although the focus of this resource book is primarily the U.S., rail travel is so prevalent in Europe that that information has been included for your convenience.

Amtrak

Specific limited seats are available for discounts. Check with the railroad or your travel agent when you know your plans. Their other special promotional and excursion fares can be a reasonable buy for any traveler. The All-Aboard America rates let you travel at will and make several stopovers. Travel in one region only, cross two regions, or go cross-country with these bargain rates.

Age Minimum: 65
Where to Buy: 800-USA-RAIL or your travel
  agent

BritRail Senior Pass

This is a good option for first-class travel in England, Scotland, and Wales. Travelers of any age should choose the normal BritRail pass. In Northern Ireland, there's the Rail

Runabout discount ticket.

Age Minimum: 60
Where to Buy: through your travel agent or the British Tourist Authority
For More Information:
BritRail (416) 929-3334 (in Canada)
(212) 575-2667

Rail Europe S
This discount is valid only if you plan to spend a considerable length of time in Europe, as it is a resident pass. However, if you plan to "reside" in Europe for at least six months, you may qualify for discounts ranging from 30 to 50 percent in 18 participating countries.

Age Minimum: women 60; men 65
Where to Buy: primary railroad stations in Europe

Eurail Pass
This well-known discount rail pass gives you considerable flexibility when traveling through Europe. However, its benefits do not extend into Great Britain. There are additional discounts for family-size groups.

Age Minimum: none — discount is not age-oriented

Where to Buy: here, before you go. For more
    information write:
Eurailpass
Box 325
Old Greenwich, CT 06879

In addition, a number of countries will extend rail discounts or passes.

Austria	Age Minimum: women 60; men 65
Bermuda	Age Minimum: 50
Canada	Age Minimum: 55
France	Age Minimum: 60
Greece	Age Minimum: 60
Italy	Age Minimum: women 62; men 65
Luxembourg	Age Minimum: 65
Portugal	Age Minimum: 60
Scandinavia	Age Minimum: 65
Switzerland	Age Minimum: none — discounts are not age-oriented
West Germany	Age Minimum: 60

Motorcoach Tours

Today's luxury motorcoaches offer one of the most relaxed ways to see the sights across the country. These spacious, well-appointed coaches provide comfortable transportation as well as an on-the-road tour base for sightseeing. Many have discovered this leisurely paced mode of travel and take trip after trip on routes that crisscross the continent. This is a splendid way to travel with a group of friends. No one is burdened with driving responsibilities, so everyone can relax and have a great time. Each of the tour companies highlighted have on-board emergency restroom facilities and make frequent rest stops for the comfort of their passengers.

Understandably, prices vary according to which tour you select (and the current state of the U.S. dollar, gas prices, and other factors). For that reason, the companies are shown simply as moderately priced ($ — less than $100 per day) or upscale ($$ — more than $100 per day) to give you an idea of the type of tour to expect.

When it is indicated to contact your travel agent, expect that the company will, at most, send you a brochure if you inquire directly. They will not compromise their relationships with travel agents to book your trip directly.

Bennett's
270 Madison Avenue
New York, NY 10016
(212) 532-5060
(Consult your travel agent)
$-$$

If Scandinavia is your destination, Bennett's has the motorcoach tours that let you get close to the people and the culture. You can see the beautiful countryside as well as the major cities by motorcoach — or by cruise ship when it fits the itinerary. You can take a trip into Russia as well, to visit Leningrad. Bennett's provides exciting "city packages" in Europe that include three nights' lodging and breakfast plus sightseeing. Another Bennett's favorite is the plan-your-own Orient and South Pacific tour.

Bennett's offers both moderately priced tours and more upscale excursions. A typical trip (regardless of price) includes a room with a private bath or shower, breakfasts, many dinners, deluxe motorcoach transportation, sightseeing with a guide, and many extras.

California Parlour Cars
1101 Van Ness Avenue
San Francisco, CA 94109
(Consult your travel agent)
$-$$

This company has been taking passengers on tours through California since 1924. They offer vacations ranging from a week to 11 days to the most popular areas of California: San Francisco, Sausalito, wine country, Pebble Beach, Carmel by the Sea, Big Sur, the Redwoods, Yosemite, and many other points of interest.

Every day is paced to let you see plenty without getting travel-weary. Every night, you will stay at a luxury hotel. Some meals are included in your package, too.

Each coach features reclining seats and expansive tinted windows for great sightseeing. The groups are small, usually no more than 36. There is a nonsmoking policy on the bus for the comfort of all passengers, but frequent rest stops allow time to smoke.

This motorcoach line and the various hotels and restaurants associated with the tours have an excellent reputation among experienced travelers. You can sample the distinctive character of the cities as well as the extraordinary natural beauty of California.

They request that you arrange your trip through your travel agent at least 14 days in advance.

Domenico Tours
751 Broadway
Bayonne, NJ 07002
(201) 823-8687
(212) 757-8687 (in New York)
800-554-8687
$

This well-known tour company offers more than 80 packages, ranging in length from 3-day jaunts to 26-day vacations. They also plan a variety of special tours centered around holidays, like a Williamsburg Christmas, festivals, such as Quebec's Winter Carnival, and special shopping sprees.

Each deluxe motorcoach carries no more than 49 passengers and is equipped with reclining seats. Domenico has its own elaborate passenger complex, Port Quinstar, in New Jersey. This facility brings a new level of comfort and convenience to passengers departing and arriving on coach tours.

Domenico stands on its reputation, built with more than a quarter of a century of service. Depending on the tour, some meals may be included. Your hotel and transportation are part of the price.

Though they built their reputation on luxury motorcoach travel, they now offer Alaskan and Caribbean cruises and train tours. To reach the origination point of your chosen tour, they will arrange your air transportation using specially priced "zoned" airfares.

Gray Line Tours
(Consult your local directory or your travel
   agent)
This group of independent bus operators form a nationwide association. Gray Line has a lock on quality city tours wherever it operates and can give you the quickest overview available of an area. Although each operator sets his or her own rates, typically anyone 50+ is accorded a 15 percent discount.

Joli Tours
49 Park Avenue, Suite A
New York, NY 10016
(212) 695-5654
800-333-JOLI
$–$$
An avid 50+ traveler is the one responsible for putting the various vacation packages together for this organization. The motorcoach line conducts tours through Switzerland, Austria, and Bavaria. You can choose two- or four-day jaunts or six-day tours. Focus on the areas that appeal to you the most, from the Alps to the elegant European cities. Depending on the tour you select, some meals are included.

Mayflower Tours
1225 Warren Avenue
PO Box 490
Downers Grove, IL 60515
(708) 960-3430 (in Illinois)
800-323-7604
$–$$

With tours departing to 70 destinations from the Chicago area, travelers can enjoy escorted visits to Florida, New England, Washington, D.C., California, Texas, the Canadian Rockies, and the Pacific Northwest, plus Hawaii, Alaska, and many other destinations. You might choose a two-, three-, or four-day mini-tour or a five-day to month-long vacation.

These experienced folks have attracted a loyal following among 50+ travelers and you are likely to find travel companions who have taken a number of Mayflower tours. Since they give a $5 Mayflower Money voucher to apply to later trips, perhaps this is not so surprising. But most would have chosen Mayflower again simply for the great value and fun.

With a guaranteed twin rate for single travelers, you will never be forced to pay higher rates, even if they cannot locate a roommate for you. Many meals are included in your package, but there also is freedom to make some dining discoveries of your own.

The tour company also offers train, air-cruise, and combination vacations to round out its extensive program. The motorcoach and train tours are fully refundable, right up to departure time, and the air-and-cruise tours have a liberal refund policy. This can be vitally important to travelers who have to make a quick schedule change.

Tauck Tours
PO Box 5027
Westport, CT 06881
(203) 226-6911
(Consult your travel agent)
$$

This company offers a wide range of tour options through the U.S., including Hawaii, and Canada. The first Tauck tour was arranged in 1925, and since then over one million people have taken their trips. Their reputation is built on excellent food (your meals are included in the price), great service, and superb hotels. Although the foliage tours in New England are among the favorites offered by this firm, Hawaii is the most popular destination. Their substantial catalog overflows with great "all-expense" vacation ideas.

See also page 329 in the "Traveling With Grandchildren" section for information on

Vistatours, which offers motorcoach trips, and the "Guided Tours" chapter, which will direct you to Grand Circle Tours and others that include motorcoach tours in their itineraries.

Buses — An Economical Option for Travel

If you have more time than budget to spend getting from city to city, the nation's bus lines offer an economical alternative. The bus system also serves some communities you cannot reach by public transportation, making bus travel a perfect choice if you prefer not to drive, fly, or rent a car.

Greyhound and Trailways
Check your local directory

The bus companies have promotional rates that vary from region to region and season to season. Check those rates first. Then show your proof of age for a 65+ discount of 10 percent for travel Monday through Thursday or 5 percent Friday, Saturday, or Sunday, if that's a better deal. You must go to the station to purchase your tickets.

Voyageur and Grey Coach
(416) 393-7911

The Canadian bus companies offer discounts of 10 to 30 percent for travelers 60+ traveling in Ontario and Quebec. Discounts vary by destination.

The Recreational Vehicle Lifestyle

There are any number of reasons to love the RV lifestyle: convenience, spontaneity, travel comfort, independence, camaraderie, and affordability, to name just a few. RV ownership is divided between budget- and schedule-conscious dual-income families raising children and 50+ adventurers who enjoy the freedom RVs allow.

The industry is well organized to give you the support you need, whether you are a complete novice or a seasoned RVer. The networks among manufacturers and owners provide every bit of information you will need to get into RV travel and enjoy it, from shopping for a vehicle to connecting with other like-minded RVers.

AARP estimates that more than nine million 50+ adventurers use RVs every year. A majority (more than 70 percent) of RV trips are made by your group. RV vacations are more cost-effective and make your travel dollars go farther. People have taken to RVs in such numbers that it is now a $4.5 billion industry!

People who want to take quick weekend trips find RVs a way to avoid hotel hassles. Folks who want to take a little longer trip find that the low camping fees allow them to stay a few extra days. RV travel actually can increase your travel dollar power by 50 to 75 percent. Aside from the savings, the RV life-style is fun, relaxed, and filled with excitement. Campground neighbors quickly become friends, and the warmth among RVers is one of the most compelling reasons people love it.

When visiting friends or relatives, there's less pressure on everyone when you bring along your own bedroom and bath. And for the snowbird who lives in his or her vehicle for weeks and months at a time in a popular Sunbelt area, an RV parked in a pleasant campground provides all of the comforts of home at a fraction of the cost.

What Is an RV?

An RV, or recreational vehicle, can be any one of a family of camping vehicles. There are two categories: towables and motorized vehicles.

- *Folding camping trailers:* these lightweight units collapse to a compact size for towing behind a car.
- *Truck campers:* these units attach to a truck bed to provide sleeping, cooking, and, in some cases, bathroom facilities.
- *Travel trailers:* these models are conventional trailers. They come in a wide variety of sizes and prices and are designed to be towed by a car or truck.
- *Park trailers:* these larger units are for seasonal living quarters. Although they can be moved, most are used as vacation homes.
- *Motorhomes:* these models are all-in-one vehicle and living quarters that often have built-in features, such as heating and air-conditioning, water, electricity, and other conveniences.
- *Van conversions:* a standard van can be customized to become a camping vehicle by adding features such as carpeting, cooking facilities, custom seats, and other comforts.

In addition to the many travel benefits of RVs, there are a variety of financial advantages as well. For example, if your RV has cooking, sleeping, and bathroom facilities, it can qualify as a second home and therefore reap tax deductions (according to the tax laws in effect at this writing).

If you don't use your RV constantly, you can rent it out to others, who might pay dealers anywhere from $20 per day for a folding camping trailer to more than $100 a day for a luxury motorhome. As a private individual, you may charge less but still realize a nice profit.

RVs traditionally have held their value, so resale prices are high. With the increased demand for RVs, used vehicles often fetch their original sales price when sold years later.

Lenders are particularly prone to give advantageous financial plans to purchasers of RVs. History has shown that RV owners are excellent risks, with fewer than 2 percent ever defaulting on their loans. The long-term, flexible financing available brings RV ownership within the reach of almost everyone.

First-time buyers can orient themselves to the industry by requesting a free information packet from the Recreation Vehicle Industry Association (RVIA), (see page 301). Another excellent resource is *The Family Camper on Wheels*, an informative video produced in cooperation with the RVIA, the National Campground Owners Association, and the Recreational Vehicles Dealers Association and endorsed by the Boy Scouts of America. It is distributed through RV dealers and other camping outlets. Contact the producers, Serendipity Communications, if the cassette is unavailable in your area (see their listing in "RV Publications" at the end of this chapter).

Rent Before You Buy

The advice you will hear universally if you have never tried RV camping is to rent before you buy. This helps orient you to the kind of vehicle that may be more appealing to you as well as give you a glimpse at the RV lifestyle. You don't have to drive the entire way. Fly to a favorite destination and pick up your RV there for a relaxed tour of the area.

You may want to contact your travel agent to arrange an RV trip. Many are finding their clients so prone to RV travel that they have added planning this type of vacation to their list of client services. Or contact one of the RV rental organizations.

Recreation Vehicle Rental Association
3251 Old Lee Highway, Suite 500
Fairfax, VA 22030
(703) 591-7130
A $5 book, *Rental Ventures,* as well as a free directory of RV rental outlets, is produced by this organization.

Cruise America
5959 Blue Lagoon Drive, Suite 170
Miami, FL 33126
800-327-7778
800-327-7799 (in Alaska and Canada)

Go Vacations
13261 Garden Grove
Garden Grove, CA 92643
(714) 740-1163
and
129 Carlingview Drive
Rexdale, Ontario, Canada M9W 5E7
(416) 674-1880
800-387-3998

Travelhome Vacations
20383 #10 Hwy
Langley, British Columbia V3A 5E8
(604) 533-1566
800-663-7848

Rental Management Systems
1201 Baldwin Park Boulevard
Baldwin Park, CA 91706
(818) 962-6907

U-Haul International
R-V Rental Division
2727 North Central
Phoenix, AZ 85036
800-821-2712

If you are checking your local area for rentals, look in the yellow pages under Recreational Vehicles — Dealers and Recreational Vehicles — Renting and Leasing.

RV rentals have high and low seasons just like hotels and resort areas. The low season is from January to the end of March and mid-October to the end of December. The lower-priced "shoulder" seasons, which connect the high and low seasons, include April to mid-July and mid-August to mid-October. The short high season runs from mid-July to mid-August. Plan to book your RV rental several months in advance, although a persistent travel agent may be able to track down a vehicle available through a cancellation.

Where To Camp

When selecting a campground, you will discover that you have the same broad range of choices as you would when looking for the ideal inn or resort. You can choose an isolated, rustic setting or an elaborate resort property.

With 20,000 campgrounds throughout the country, there's always somewhere new to explore.

CAMPGROUND ASSOCIATIONS

National Campground Owners Association
11307 Sunset Hills Road, Suite B-7
Reston, VA 22090
(703) 471-0143

Individual states have their own campground associations. Contact the RVIA for the pertinent information by calling (703) 620-6003 in the East or (714) 532-1688 in the West. For camping information, especially for the beginner, there is a Go Camping America Hotline. Call 800-47 SUNNY.

NATIONAL AND STATE PARKS AND LANDS

U.S. Government Printing Office
Superintendent of Documents
Washington, D.C. 20402

Request the *National Park Camping Guide* (stock number 024-005-01028-9), available for $3.50. Although the more popular campgrounds at Yosemite or Yellowstone may be crowded at peak season, there are many less-crowded areas where you can camp. There's also the *Lesser Known Areas of the National Park System,* for $1.50. With more than 350 parks and 440 campgrounds, you can discover some less-populated areas nestled in scenic paradises.

U.S. Forest Service
Department of Agriculture
Office of Information
PO Box 2417
Washington, D.C. 20013

There are more than 6,000 campgrounds in over 150 national forests filled with hiking trails, streams, and lakes. A free listing of the various forest supervisors (number FS-65) is available on request. Each supervisor has current information on the campsites in the forest under his or her direction.

Bureau of Land Management (BLM)
Public Affairs Office
1800 C Street NW
Washington, D.C. 20240

There are 300 million acres of land where you can hunt, fish, hike, and camp. Contact the BLM for camping information.

U.S. Army Corps of Engineers (USACE)
Projects

If you love camping near oceans, lakes,

or rivers, you may enjoy one of the 53,000 campsites developed by the USACE. Contact the district office in the area you plan to visit.

CAMPING AT A DISCOUNT

Typically rates are low for campsites, and any special rates are on a per-property basis. However, with the KOA Value Card or a Good Sam card, you can travel across the country saving at least 10 percent every night. Secure a Golden Age pass if you are 62+ and gain free admission to the national park system or wildlife refuges for a lifetime. You must show proof of age and U.S. citizenship.

You will receive as much as a 50-percent discount on overnight stays and other park-user fees and services. You must apply in person at the entrance to any park that charges a fee or at any of the following offices: National Park Service, U.S. Fish and Wildlife Service, National Forest Service, Bureau of Land Management, Bureau of Reclamation, or U.S. Army Corps of Engineers. The National Parks Service Office of Public Inquiry is (202) 343-4747.

American Hiking Society
1015 Thirty-first Street NW
Washington, D.C. 20007
(703) 385-3252

There is a variety of volunteer services you can provide in the national parks and forests for which you will receive free camping in exchange. These opportunities are outlined in *Helping Out in the Outdoors,* a $3 booklet available from the American Hiking Society.

RV Clubs and Associations

In the RV world, there are two organizations you should know about:

Recreation Vehicle Industry Association
  (RVIA)
1896 Preston White Drive
PO Box 2999
Reston, VA 22090
(703) 620-6003
and
Western Office
1748 West Katella Avenue, Suite 108
Orange, CA 92667
(714) 532-1688

These friendly people are the primary source for all information pertaining to the

RV industry, from the manufacturers who make parts and vehicles, to the campground owners, to the RVers who enjoy the lifestyle. They can introduce you to the industry with a free packet of information (as mentioned earlier). They can help you shop for your vehicle by providing a schedule of the RV and camping shows in your area. Anyone who's anyone in the RV world knows and is known by this group. They will be happy to share their knowledge and expertise to make your RV life more pleasurable. You can request their free *Catalog of Publications About the RV Lifestyle* to learn about everything from buying tips to RV maintenance.

Good Sam Club
29901 Agoura Road
Agoura, CA 91301
(818) 991-4980
800-234-3450

Over one million RVers are members of the Good Sam Club, and with good reason. This group provides a card good for 10 percent discounts at Sam-selected campgrounds. In addition, a magazine gives you good information about the RV lifestyle and planned trips. As a service organization, they also provide valuable insurance, an emergency road service (generally unavailable for RVs through other sources), mail forwarding, and discounts on a variety of products and services. They'll help you with lost credit cards, pets, and keys. In short, Good Sam is the guardian angel of RVers traveling across the country. And as a group, they have a great time together.

CLUBS FOR SINGLES

There are single, widowed, or divorced RVers who want to enjoy the company of others on the road without the obligation of becoming part of a couple to enjoy the group. Neither of the two organizations listed next are designed as a dating service; in fact, you will lose your membership if you find a partner inside or outside of one club. Nevertheless, you can have the security of traveling with a group and have the fun of camping with friends, receiving newsletters, and joining planned trips and other benefits.

Loners of America (LOA)
Lorraine Shannon
Route 2, Box 85D
Ellsnore, MO 63937
(in summer)
or

191 Villa Del Rio Boulevard
Boca Raton, FL 33937
(in winter)

Loners on Wheels (LOW)
Dick March
808 Lester Street
Poplar Bluff, MO 63901

CLUBS FOR SPECIFIC PRODUCT OWNERS

Virtually every manufacturer of RVs sponsors a club or association for its owners. When you purchase your vehicle, inquire about which organization is available to connect you with other owners. RVIA has the list as well.

For companies that modify RVs for those with physical disabilities, refer to the chapter "The Handicapped Traveler."

RV Publications

There seems to be an endless array of regional, state, club, and special interest publications for the RV traveler, plus helpful repair manuals and catalogs for products you may need. RVIA is your best source for a list of these publications. Many of the books are sold through its own offices. The catalog is free (see the address listing on page 301). Here are a few of the selections offered:

The Family Camper on Wheels (forty minute video; $19.95 plus $2.50 shipping and handling, from Serendipity Communications, 50 Briar Hollow Lane, Houston, Texas 77092)

Living Aboard Your Recreational Vehicle: A Guide to the Fulltime Life on Wheels, by Gordon and Janet Groene

Mobile Retirement Handbook: A Complete Guide to Living and Traveling in an RV, by Jurgen Hesse

RV Repair and Maintenance Manual, by John Thompson

Woodall's RV Buyer's Guide

Guided Tours: Land, Sea, and Air

Tour Operators and Agents

Your notion of escorted tours may bring up visions of tourists, each with a name tag and camera swinging, being herded like a flock of sheep through tourist traps of the world in the "If it's Tuesday it must be . . ." tradition. Take another look. Today's more sophisticated tour operators market to specific groups, either by budget or by interest. Some naturally draw 50+ travelers simply because that group has both the time and money to enjoy the world's most interesting places. Others target the 50+ market with appealing cost-conscious rates or itineraries that make touring a pleasure instead of a strain.

To simplify your planning, the travel companies featured here have been divided into two main groups: those who plan trips to exotic places and those who design trips specifically for the mature market. Except where noted, your travel agent can arrange your trips with the tour company.

It is true that some of the more deluxe tours cost as much (or more) as many people make in a year. They are included here for the simple reason that if you are one who dreams of travel, the dreams may as well be about the very best available. And if you are among the privileged few for whom money literally is no object, it would be a shame if these sensational epic travel adventures were to escape your notice.

The pricing guidelines are subject to the fluctuating dollar and many other factors. However, to help guide you, the $ designation is for moderately priced tours (around $100 per day) and the $$ designation is for the higher-priced, deluxe tours (starting at $100 and ranging upward of several hundred dollars per day).

Exotic Destinations

Abercrombie & Kent International
1520 Kensington Road, Suite 212
Oak Brook, IL 60521
(708) 954-2944 (in Illinois)
800-323-7308
$$

Catering to the world's most sophisticated traveler, A and K was founded to create custom travel in East Africa. The company still provides tailor-made planning as well as unparalleled tours to the world's most exotic destinations. Inspired by travel brochures as enticing as the *National Geographic,* you can plot your trips to the Orient, the Galápagos Islands, Australia, or Nepal. Or select one of the trips that will take you to the country houses or château hotels in Britain, Ireland, or France.

If you're feeling particularly adventurous, one of their safaris may suit your mood. There is the traditional tented safari or the flying boat safaris (fly/water cruises). Either gives you a view of Africa that you won't soon forget.

For a truly once-in-a-lifetime experience — "to see the master works of man and nature" — take the Royal Air Tour, on which you will visit such diverse locales as Bora-Bora, the Masai Mara Game Reserve, and Mount Kenya. Flights between destinations are aboard a specially modified L-1011 that has been customized to accommodate just 88 passengers (not the usual 344), complete with a lounge. For the majority, this kind of trip is a fantasy (more than $1,000 a day for the month-long adventure). Yet A and K, true to their promise of only the best, provides sensational travel for the elite. The same quality and attention to detail is more affordable on their shorter, less-elaborate journeys.

Also see A and K in the "Cruises" and "Trains" sections (pages 247, 255, and 270).

American Express Vacations
(Call your local independent American
  Express travel agent)
$$

The company that throws a security blanket around the world for travelers is also one of the leading tour planners. Choose one of its group tours or a "free-lance" trip for personal exploration of Europe, Great Britain, and other destinations.

Travcoa
(Consult your travel agent)
$$

Another round-the-world-by-private-jet fantasy tour is available from Travcoa. A privileged group of 60 takes a 36-day journey that includes Moscow, Africa, India, Tibet, Hong Kong, New Zealand, and the South Pacific. Every stop along the way has luxury accommodations waiting. Lecturers give you insight into the cultures you will encounter. You will enjoy gourmet dining and vintage wines. Nothing has been spared to insure that you will have the trip of your life. For example, you can view wildlife in the Masai Mara from a hot-air balloon, weather permitting.

For an in-depth, luxurious trip, Travcoa offers tours to the Orient, the South Pacific, Africa, Egypt and the Holy Lands, India, Western Europe, and Eastern Europe. Each of these tours is limited to an intimate group of 25 on trips lasting anywhere from 9 to 52 days. Trips are all-inclusive, with sumptuous meals, wines, and other extras. Prominent lecturers join the tours to provide the educational background that makes the travel more interesting.

Classic's Tours International
625 North Michigan Avenue, Suite 900
Chicago, IL 60611
(312) 642-2400
800-828-8222
$$

Africa has always held a fascination for serious travelers. Classic's has been known as an innovative travel planner to satisfy the demands of sophisticated travelers. The ordinary simply will not do for the typical Classic's client. In Africa, there are four categories of travel arrangements: classic safaris, featuring 10-, 14-, 17-, or 18-day jaunts; a la carte safaris that let you get off the beaten track; foreign independent travel, for custom itineraries; and special interest tours, for groups wanting to pursue travel interests ranging from golf to camel safaris.

Classic's has expanded its operation to include other exotic destinations: Egypt, Morocco, and Turkey. Whether cruising the Nile, shopping in a colorful bazaar, or listening to a lecture on ancient civilization, you will enjoy luxurious accommodations every stop along the way.

Club Med
(Contact your travel agent)
$$

If you are interested in learning or pursuing a sport such as skiing or scuba diving or you plan to take grandchildren along, Club Med has a few programs in its primarily youth-oriented market of interest.

Safariworld
425 Madison Avenue
New York, NY 10017
(212) 486-0505
800-366-0505
$$

When your heart longs to explore Africa, to stay in the traditional lodges and observe the wildlife roaming freely, but you must be conscious of budgets, the more moderately priced Safariworld may hold the key to your dreams. On these safaris, you will stay in many of the same spots and see the same sights as you would with the super-luxurious tour companies, but at a price within reach of many more travelers. Tour prices include airfare from New York to your destination as well as all meals.

Because the ground travel can be rough, Safariworld also offers a gentler Wings Over Mara program so that you can fly over, not drive over, the distances required to reach the more-remote locations. They have found this to be particularly popular with those for whom bumpy overland travel would be uncomfortable or tiring.

Tours of Distinction
141 East 44th Street
New York, NY 10017
(212) 661-4680
$$

Plan a "tour group" as small as you and your spouse to exotic destinations in India, Nepal, Bhutan, Burma, Thailand, or Singapore. Tours of Distinction tours last anywhere from 8 to 24 days and include traditional sights as well as contemporary attractions. You can even book passage on the Palace on Wheels, a 12-coach train dating back to the 1920s, when the maharajas traveled in luxury throughout the country.

These tours are suited to your personal interests. Some are more oriented to the native wildlife, others feature such breathtaking sights as the Taj Mahal. Many meals, as well as sightseeing tours, are included.

Target Market Tours

The tour operators who are after your business have a wide variety of trips available in every price range.

AARP Travel Service
800-227-7737

This travel service, which is for members only, provides tours, cruises, educational expeditions, luxury vacations, and more through Olson-Travelworld. AARP has your specific lifestyle considerations in mind, since they cater exclusively to the 50+ market. This is one of those services that you must contact directly, not through your local travel agent.

Adriatic Tours
691 West Tenth Street
San Pedro, CA 90731
(213) 548-1446
$–$$

This company specializes in tours to Italy, Yugoslavia, and Russia. With programs designed to capture your attention, Adriatic's tours feature lectures, dances, candlelight dinners, and even a health improvement vacation. Guests can use the facilities at the renowned Thallassotherapia Institute at Opatija (for heart, lung, and rheumatic diseases) and at the Dr. Orest Zunkovic Allergological Center in Hvar (for bronchial asthma and allergies).

Airfare from the U.S., accommodations, breakfasts and dinners, ground transportation (depending on the tour), plus lots of extras are included in these moderately priced packages.

AJS Travel Consultants
(Call your travel agent)
$–$$

The 50+ market is a specialty with this company. Look to them for excellent tours to Israel, Switzerland, and Italy.

American Jewish Congress
International Travel Program
15 East 84th Street
New York, NY 10028
(212) 879-4588 (in New York City)
(516) 752-1186 (in Long Island)
(914) 328-0018 (in Westchester and Rockland)

(212) 879-4588 (collect, from the rest of New York)
800-221-4694
$$

With more than 32 years of experience in travel, the American Jewish Congress has gained an excellent reputation for travel value. Their international tours have been highly acclaimed. Of special interest are the trips to Israel for singles over 55. Prices include airfare and some meals. These tours are available to members only; make application when you reserve your trip if you are not yet a member.

Golden Age Travellers Club
Pier 27, The Embarcadero
San Francisco, CA 94111
(415) 296-0151
800-258-8880
$-$$

This club has been around for more than 20 years to help 50+ travelers get the best deals available. Through a bimonthly newsletter, members learn of cruises, land tours, budget trips, and exotic vacations. They also provide a roommate-match service to help lower costs for single travelers. A modest annual membership fee covers their services and publication.

Grand Circle Travel
347 Congress Street
Boston, MA 02210
(617) 350-7500
800-221-2610
$–$$

These pros have been planning travel adventures for the 50+ traveler for decades. They offer Alaskan Princess cruises and CruiseTours as well as tours throughout the world. Seasonal bargains can run approximately $100 per day, including airfare and some meals. Call them directly for information and free brochures, such as their concise *Going Abroad: 101 Tips for the Mature Traveler.*

Haddon Holidays
1120 Route 75, Suite 375
Mount Laurel, NJ 08054
800-257-7488
$–$$

Haddon specializes in tours to Hawaii. Special prices on trips as well as a certificate for a hefty discount on future travel are available for clients 60+.

National Retirement Concepts
Division of Lampert Tours
1454 North Wieland Court
Chicago, IL 60610
(312) 951-2866
$-$$

Preview a variety of retirement villages through the Quest for the Best tours offered by this organization. This is especially beneficial for those considering relocation to the Sunbelt. You will have the chance to see developments in Arizona, Arkansas, North Carolina, South Carolina, or Florida. While staying in first-class lodgings, you will be visiting a variety of villages and communities in the chosen area. The 7-night trips include 13 meals, van transportation at the destination, taxes, baggage handling, and tips. You will have the benefit of getting a feel for the whole area while gathering enough material to make an informed decision about your relocation plans.

Saga International Holidays
120 Boylston Street
Boston, MA 02116
(617) 451-6808
800-343-0273 (sales)
800-366-7242 (brochure hotline)
$-$$

Saga Holidays is the industry leader in the special interest, 60+ travel market. They began in 1950 as a small company catering to British pensioners, but today their operation takes travelers throughout the world, provides financial services, and is involved in publishing and in retirement housing.

Count on Saga for satisfying tours to both North and South America, Australia, Asia, Africa, and Europe. Saga offers lecture tours, grandparent-child programs, singles departures, and more. The Saga Holidays Club offers discounts and a friendly travel group. Whether you want to see the beautiful gardens of England or shop for folk art in South America, Saga undoubtedly has a tour to suit you. If there is a definitive commercial travel group serving the travel needs of those 50+, this is it.

Since the typical tour package includes airfare, lodgings, and many meals, most trips qualify as moderately priced adventures.

Senior Escorted Tours
PO Box 400
Cape May Court House, NJ 08010
(609) 465-4011
800-222-1254
$–$$

You can count on the personal touch with

this tour group, because the president, Gilbert Sinkway, plans and escorts most of the tours personally. Enjoy cruises, Europe, Canada, Florida, and other adventures. For the flexibility of independent travel, you can plan your own getaway, with rates you might expect for group travel. You get to choose the options that appeal to you rather than paying for those you won't use.

Yugotours
350 Fifth Avenue
New York, NY 10118
(212) 563-2400
800-223-5298
$

The Prime of Your Life Program provides an appealing way to visit Italy, Greece, Yugoslavia, or Russia. You have a choice of full-length vacations or minivacations. You can even choose to base yourself at a Yugoslavian resort and take day trips to explore the surrounding countryside rather than be on the move constantly. Targeted to the 50+ market, the prices include airfare, some meals, and many bonus activities, such as dances, entertainment, sightseeing expeditions, and more.

Extended-stay rates are incredibly low and include airfare, hotel, two meals daily, sightseeing, and luggage handling. Providing that economic and political changes do not spoil the fun, you could vacation for less money than it would cost to live at home for the same length of time! Look into this one, especially if your roots are in the Adriatic. This could be a sensational buy, providing that you make sure the standard of living in a different culture meets your expectations.

Also see the "Motorcoach Tours" section (pages 283-290) for additional experienced tour operators, such as Mayflower and Domenico. There are also several outstanding tour planners listed in the "Traveling With Grandchildren" section (pages 326-330). Check in the "Clubs and Associations" chapter for the Retired Officers Association, which offers travel services (see page 369).

Solo Travel

Single travelers have a special set of concerns. One practical problem is the extra expense involved in traveling alone — single-accommodation supplements on tours, at hotels, and on cruises. The second problem is emotional. Some people are not comfortable braving it on their own and prefer the company of a group of compatible traveling companions; yet the prospect of being one of a handful of singles among many couples can be intimidating. While single-only tours are an alternative, some may be looking for the opportunity to find a partner while others may adamantly prefer an atmosphere free of dating pressure.

There are solutions. Elsewhere in the book, you will find information about the Merry Widows Dance Cruises and a fun-filled Premier Cruise (see the "Cruises" section, starting on page 207). Singles on the RV circuit can find companionship without pressure to be matched up in either the Loners on Wheels or Loners of America groups (see "The Recreational Vehicle Lifestyle," starting on page 291).

An alternative idea for saving money if you are traveling crosscountry by yourself is to consult the discount sections, which can point you to lodgings with room night prices rather than the typical per-person, double-occupancy rates. You might also investigate the suite hotels, such as Compri or Embassy Suites, which have many single guests, often business travelers, who may congregate for companionship in the central restaurant and lounge areas. In this protected environment, you won't feel awkward speaking to strangers, and sharing a table for dinner is not uncommon.

Several tour planning companies already

mentioned at the beginning of this chapter, including Mayflower Tours, Saga Holidays, and Grand Circle Travel, are sensitive to your needs. They will help you plan a suitable vacation with a reduced single supplement or provide a match service to find you a roommate.

There are a few travel companies that specialize in singles-only travel:

Suddenly Single Tours
161 Dreiser Loop
New York, NY 10475
(212) 379-8800

Every year this organization plans numerous first-class trips for singles who are looking to begin new friendships. The deluxe tours include transportation, meals, guides, first-class hotels, and tickets to operas, museums, or other attractions planned for like-minded travelers. There are no double-occupancy rooms, just private accommodations with no single-supplement fees to pay. The trips range from jaunts to domestic locations, such as New Orleans, Las Vegas, or New York, to guided tours of international destinations.

This can be the ideal environment for people abruptly left single to find themselves, or orient themselves to a new role, while discovering new travel adventures with new friends. There is a sensitivity to the special emotional needs of a person newly single. It's a comfortable atmosphere in which extra care and attention are provided along with the security of traveling with other sophisticated adults.

Solo Flights
127 South Compo Road
Westport, CT 06880
(203) 226-9993

This travel agency specializes in single travel, particularly for the 50+ traveler. Founder Betty Sobel keeps track of the best cruises, tours, and hotels to suit the needs of single clients. The agency knows the places and cruises that defer to singles and the cozy couples-only places you want to avoid.

You can plan a solo flight for a reclusive journey or join one of the groups taking off all over the world. Plan a weekend getaway or a long vacation. Since this agency arranges travel for a wide range of clients with many interests, you don't have to conform to any particular "single traveler" mold to enjoy yourself. Out-of-town clients are invited to call during evening hours to take advantage of low long distance rates.

Refer also to the "Tour Operators and

Agents" section, which lists the American Jewish Congress (see pages 314-315). Of special interest are the trips to Israel for singles over 55.

If you like to travel but prefer to be matched with a suitable roommate, one of the clubs that provide matching services may hold the key for you.

Golden Companions
PO Box 754
Pullman, WA 99163
(208) 883-5052

With members ranging in age from 50 to 86, this travel companion network is for active, energetic travelers (more than half are avid walkers). The $40 six-month or $60 annual membership will bring you profiles on the 800-plus and growing membership, a bimonthly newsletter, travel discounts, plus vacation home exchange opportunities. Local members often organize themselves for get-togethers through a designated "social contact" in the area. Founder and president Joanne R. Buteau reports that the service has resulted in many successful matches, and even a few marriages, since its inception in 1987.

Partners-in-Travel
PO Box 491145
Los Angeles, CA 90049
(213) 476-4869

Started as a newsletter to post notices for single travelers seeking companions, this publication now includes valuable travel tidbits you might have overlooked in the major papers or magazines. The accent is on the 50+ traveler, many of whom are looking for partners willing to spend a substantial amount of time exploring the world. Subscription rates are $25 for six months, $40 for a year.

Travel Companion Exchange
PO Box 833
Amityville, NY 11701
(516) 454-0880

Although this well-known organization matches travelers ranging in age from 18 to 80+, the majority are 50+. Members include those who have RVs and others who have passes for free or reduced travel (by virtue of their professions). Still others participate in a "hosting exchange" program sponsored by the group, which lets you visit with members in their own home cities. The rates vary according to the type of membership: associate membership, for those seeking same-sex companions, 6 months for $36 or one year for $60; VIP membership, for those looking for same-sex or opposite-sex companions, 6 months for $66, one year for $120; newsletter subscription only, 6 months for $24 or one year for $36.

Traveling With Grandchildren

Recently, a TV character, faced with the prospect of becoming a grandmother, reflected the feelings of many when she declared that having grandchildren was fine, it was being a grandparent that was a problem.

For the active 50+ individual, the time-weary image of grandma or grandpa rocking on the front porch, with grandchildren at their feet munching home-baked cookies, simply does not apply. Today's grandparents are more likely to be trekking up mountains or exploring country backroads on bicycles, having traded the apron and overalls for sweats and running shoes.

Since families are scattered across the country, frequent visits no longer are feasible. When grandparents live great distances from their grandchildren, sometimes the solution to get that elusive quality time with the kids is to take a vacation together. To plan such a trip, find a travel agent who specializes in family travel.

Your own agency may have recently developed a family travel department or assigned a family travel counselor. They have access to the new generation of tour wholesalers who market tours specifically for grandparents and grandchildren or family-oriented programs that grandparents can enjoy with their grandkids.

In general these are not budget-priced trips. You can easily see from the destinations of some — China, Russia, Paris, Hawaii — that the location alone dictates higher rates. If budget is a concern, look to the motorcoach tours designed for families, since these tend to be more moderately priced. It is the time spent with the children, not the cost, that will be remembered in the years to come. Choose an adventure based on your financial comfort level to make sure that you enjoy the trip, too!

Grandparent-Child Adventures

Grandtravel
Division of the Ticket Counter
6900 Wisconsin Avenue, Suite 706
Chevy Chase, MD 20815
(301) 986-0790 (in Maryland)
800-247-7651

A pioneer in the growing grand family travel

concept, this company offers small group tours (about 20 participants) during the summer that are especially for grandparents and grandchildren. Although this is a travel agency, you can book their special Grandtravel packages through your own travel agent if you prefer. The trips, designed by a team of teachers, psychologists, and travel experts, are the kind of memory-making vacations that have lifelong impact for both the adults and the children. Much of the stress and pressure that could ruin a trip with children is reduced in these planned tours.

Grandtravel has given grandparents (and surrogate grandparents) the chance to give a special gift for a birthday, graduation, or other special occasion to a favorite child.

The hallmarks of Grandtravel are itineraries that encourage learning in a casual, unstructured atmosphere, private time for adults and children to share, and peer activities so that the adults get some adult company and children get supervised playtime with other children.

You can plan domestic trips to Washington, D.C., the Southwest (to learn about Indians), canyon country, the West, California's Pacific Coast, and Alaska. International trips may take you to castles in England, along the canals of Holland, to the outback in Australia, or on a safari, among other adventures.

This is a carefully developed concept with impressive pretrip preparation materials.

Saga Holidays
120 Boylston Street
Boston, MA 02116
800-343-0273 (sales)
800-366-7242 (brochure hotline)

Experts in senior travel, Saga (see page 317-318) has special grandparent-grandchild trips to Disney World.

Schilling Travel
722 Second Avenue South
Minneapolis, MN 55402
(612) 332-1100
800-992-1903

Special programs are developed for grandparents and grandchildren for tours to the Soviet Union, England, and Ireland.

Vistatours
Division of Frontier Travel
1923 North Carson Street, Suite 105
Carson City, NV 89701
(702) 882-2100
800-647-0800

This motorcoach company is finding enthusiastic multigenerational clients for their specially planned tours of such areas as South Dakota; Washington, D.C.; Williamsburg, Virginia; and Texas. Many events are designed to be shared, but time is built-in for privacy. For example, the South Dakota Adventure lets the children camp outdoors one night, under supervision, so that the grandparents can have some time to themselves. The next morning, the children prepare a campfire breakfast for their grandparents.

Family Tours

While the following groups promote tours that may be intriguing for a grandparent-child trip, they also are designed to include young families, single parent-child vacations, and a variety of other family groups.

Families Welcome
21 West Colony Place, Suite 140
Durham, NC 27705
(919) 489-2555
800-326-0724

The popular City Kids programs provide family fun in Paris, London, and New York. Packages include "clustered" sightseeing plans, which schedule visits to a variety of attractions, playgrounds, and restaurants all in a single area to keep everyone happy and not overtired from transit rides. Welcome kits give family-oriented information, such as a list of local, reputable babysitting services.

Family Faire
420 Fifth Avenue South, Suite E
Edmonds, WA 98020
(206) 774-6625
800-677-4FUN

West Coast and Hawaiian destinations are the first packages offered by this wholesaler, but plans are in development to expand the program. Age-rated activities are included in the itineraries to make the most of the attractions in the selected destination. Grandparents will be given a "Fun Guide" for their destination including helpful directions, a restaurant guide, the location of pharmacies and other valuable insider information. The computerized material is updated frequently.

International Family Adventures
PO Box 172
New Canaan, CT 06840
(203) 972-3842

For international travel adventures, this company offers trips to China, the Soviet Union, Australia, and Africa. The typical tour lasts two weeks and has activities suitable for children ranging from 6 to 16 years of age.

R.F.D. Travel Corporation
5201 Johnson Drive
Mission, KS 66205
(913) 722-2333
800-365-5359

This company has entered the market with the American Heritage Tour through Pennsylvania, Washington, D.C., and on into Virginia. They also are beginning multi-generational tours, such as the one planned around the Rose Parade.

Rascals in Paradise
650 Fifth Street, No. 505
San Francisco, CA 94107
(415) 978-9800
800-U-RASCAL

This company focuses on tropical destinations, with an accent on such activities as scuba diving. One particular feature is the Exotic Classroom Series, which are teacher-escorted tours to Mexico, the Galápagos, Fiji, Bali, Australia, and Africa. Some children can earn school credit to compensate for being taken out of the classroom.

Smithsonian Institution
1100 Jefferson Drive SW
Washington, D.C. 20560
(202) 357-4700

Through the National Associates Program, families can join tours to study ecology and other subjects. Programs change, so check on current schedules and subjects.

Refer also to the "Tour Operators and Agents" section for the American Jewish Congress (page 314), which plans family tours of Israel in addition to other special trips. They can arrange to have your grandchild's bar mitzvah or bas mitzvah on the trip.

See also American Wilderness Adventures in the "Live and Learn" section (page 44) and their Old West Dude Ranch division in "The Ranch Experience" (page 55) for more potential adventures with the grandchildren.

Check out the "Cruises" section (starting on page 207) for such family-friendly lines as Premier, the official cruise line of Walt Disney World.

Other Multigeneration Options

Refer to the section on traditional hotels for several excellent choices for family reunions or multigenerational vacations. Such properties as Tides Inn, Grove Park Inn, and the other elegant family resorts provide enough activities to satisfy all age levels. There's a warm welcome at these resorts that makes families feel at home. You also may want to review the chapter "Do Something, Learn Something Vacations" (pages 25-77) to discover the ranches and ski resorts which might be attractive to younger members of your family. Don't forget how much children love to camp. If you have an RV, traveling can be relaxed and fun with children, snacks are readily available, and at the campgrounds, there's plenty of room to run off steam.

Hotels are becoming increasingly aware of the need to cater to families. Camp Hyatt features supervised activities under the direction of qualified counselors. Hilton has opened a youth center in its Las Vegas property to provide age-appropriate activities under adult supervision. Resort locations that are likely to attract families, such as ski areas or oceanside properties, are creating structured programs to give adults a break and to provide interesting activities or entertainment for the children. Even exclusive city hotels are responding with extras for the kids, such as welcome kits, which tell about child-oriented features of the city. Your travel agent can be the best source of up-to-date information about amenities for children, which constantly are being added and enhanced and can make your trip with grandchildren manageable and fun for all of you.

Check in the hotel discount section. There are several hotels that allow you to extend your age-specific discount to cover other family members staying with you as you travel across the country together.

Resources

Airline Information and Discounts

The airlines want your business, and they are willing to compete for it. They recognize that you are among the affluent who may fly numerous times a year for pleasure or business. Many have programs designed specifically for you. Their marketing departments know that you may have more flexibility in your schedule and have the option to travel more frequently. Their programs reflect how much they want to capture your business.

The information provided here is intended to help you discover the best opportunities for your particular travel needs. With the industry in constant flux, these programs may change, so it's always wise to confirm.

To make your trip as pleasant and economical as possible, keep these important points in mind as you make your travel plans:

• Although the senior programs outlined are designed to save you money, remember that you can enjoy the programs open to the general public as well. Many senior programs are designed not just to save you money but also to fill seats that otherwise may be empty on less-traveled routes or during less-popular times. Those limitations may not fit with your plans for a certain trip. Let your travel agent shop for the schedule and rate that suit you best.

- Many people are nervous about buying the no-refund tickets, despite their outstanding prices. Don't worry. If you should have a death in the family or a serious illness that prevents you from completing the trip as planned, an airline normally will issue a refund, providing that you have proof, such as a letter from your doctor. When you make your reservations, discuss the airline's policy.

  If you must cancel, be patient with the airline if they press for written documentation or if processing takes some time. The airlines are sensitive to your personal problems, but at the same time they must protect themselves against fraud and abuse, which ultimately costs the consumer.

- Treat yourself to the free luxury of a travel agency. Their services cost you absolutely nothing and they can save you time and money. Using their computers, travel agents can scan for the best times and rates at a glance. Travel agents can register you into their client files and note all of your personal travel information, such as smoking or nonsmoking preferences, food restrictions, whether you prefer aisle or window seats, and your frequent flyer numbers for various airlines. Once in the computer, every trip can be checked against your personal file to ensure that you get the service you want en route and the frequent flyer credit for your flight mileage.

• Special meals are one of the extras you may find the most beneficial. Most airlines offer alternative meals, and even people without special dietary restrictions often treat themselves to fruit plates, seafood salads, or vegetarian meals. Depending on the airline, you may have simply diabetic or low-sodium, low-fat options, or you may find a tremendous variety including kosher foods, vegetarian selections, and more. All airlines require at least twenty-four hours' notice to meet your special meal requests.

The trend, however, is to offer fewer meals, replacing them with snacks or no food whatsoever. Packing a piece of fruit, granola bars, or single-serving soup packets may help you maintain your blood sugar level and keep your moods under control.

If you have any physical limitations:

- If you need any kind of special help or consideration, give the airline advance notice and arrive as early as possible (about an hour before the flight) so that the airline is able to handle your requests without interfering with other passengers.
- If you have a disability or simply prefer not to deal with the stress of making a fast connection, make sure you allow for extra time between planes. An hour or two would not be unreasonable. With delayed flights, minimum connection times, and changed gates, passengers sometimes must run a marathon between airport terminals to make their planes. You do not want that kind of pressure to spoil your trip. Better to have a cup of coffee during a leisurely wait between flights.
- Request wheelchair assistance or transportation by "people mover" between gates if walking is too strenuous. You do not have to be handicapped to request this service. Heart patients or anyone needing to avoid the hassles of airport crowds can ask for this special help.
- If you or someone traveling with you has a wheelchair, ask that it be stowed conveniently so that you will not have a long wait at your destination. If you have an electric or battery-powered chair, notify the airline

in advance in case your chair needs special handling. Some chair batteries contain a caustic acid that is illegal for the airlines to carry. If you know in advance, you can make alternative plans.

- Seeing Eye and Hearing Ear dogs must be registered for your flight when you make your reservations. Your dog must be confirmed by the airline, since the number of dogs on any given flight may be limited.
- Since the airlines are concerned with the safety of all passengers, anyone with a disability can expect a special briefing on emergency procedures that take his or her condition into account. Disabled persons generally are not seated near the emergency exits.

Club Rooms

Flying can be strenuous. Many people enjoy the luxury of having the relative quiet and calm of the private clubs offered by the various airlines. In these lounges, you normally can expect to find a receptionist who can issue boarding passes, cash checks, and help you with certain travel plans. You will find telephones, photocopying machines (in many locations), and computers (in limited locations). Conference rooms are available for meetings.

Originally designed to cater to the business traveler, leisure travelers now frequent these lounges to get away from the crowds. As a member, you usually can count on bringing your traveling companion with you, but don't try to send someone with your card; memberships are not transferable.

Business travelers often belong to more than one club, but you may find that for your travel needs, a single airline will serve most of the airports you use. These lounges are a particularly welcome sight in foreign airports when you feel lost or disoriented and unable to speak the language.

It's easy to join. Your travel agent can arrange membership for most clubs, or you can pick up an application at a ticket counter or club room. Prices for individuals range from about $150 to $200 per year, with 3-year and lifetime memberships available. Spouses can join for a modest extra fee, usually ranging from $25 to $50.

Several airlines have Senior Lifetime Memberships, which cost approximately $600 to $875 (additional for spouse), depending on the airline. The toll-free reservation numbers below will reach a representative who can tell you the airline's current rates.

For Senior Lifetime Memberships call:

American Airlines — Admirals Club (60+),
   800-433-7300

Pan American — Clipper Club (60+),
   800-221-1111

United Airlines — Red Carpet Club (62+,
   associated with their Silver Wings
   Program), 800-241-6522

U.S. Air — U.S. Air Club (65+),
   800-428-4322

If your favorite airline is not listed, call
and ask whether they have begun offering
a senior rate for the club membership. Many
are looking for ways to further enhance
their services to you, the affluent (frequent)
50+ flier. However, the regular rates are
not unreasonable for people who fly regularly, so choose the clubs on the basis of
convenience, if not price.

Discounts

The discounts listed here are current at
publication and should be reconfirmed when
you make your reservations. Discounts are
the easiest way to get a better rate, regardless
of when you fly. In some cases, you can
use your discount even on reduced rates.
In other cases the discount applies to regular
fares only.

For the lowest fare, you'll probably have

to abide by some conditions. The most common restrictions include days you must and days you cannot travel, staying over Saturday night, booking far in advance or at the last minute, plus stiff penalties for changes.

Some programs are specifically designed for those who can make last-minute travel plans. The coupon programs listed have many restrictions, because the airlines are selling leftover seats close to the departure date. If your plans can fit their plan, both you and the airline win — you get inexpensive travel, and they fill otherwise empty seats.

We have listed only the major terms of these programs, because they contain a lot of small print filled with legal jargon. Nevertheless, it is worth the effort to investigate these programs, because they offer unparalleled miles-per-dollar travel bargains.

As with all travel plans, it is wise to consult with your travel agent. Their computers are programmed to give them instant access to current information.

Destinations are listed to give a general idea of the extent of the airline's reach. Complete routes can be obtained by calling your travel agent or the airline's 800 number. All prices listed are subject to change without notice.

Air Canada
800-422-6232
Discounts: Each flight has a published senior fare, not a consistent percentage discount.
Conditions:
Must be 65 years or older
Must make reservations fourteen days in advance
Must stay over Saturday night
Must return within six months
For Florida only:
Must be 60 years or older
Must fly from Florida on Tuesday, Wednesday, Thursday, or Friday
Must fly to Florida on Sunday, Monday, Tuesday, or Wednesday
Cancellation or change fee of $39

Alaska Airlines
800-426-0333
Discounts: 10 percent on all fares including seven- and fourteen-day advance discounts
Conditions: must be 62 years or older
Bonus: one companion of any age can fly for the same fare

Alitalia Airlines
800-223-5730
Discounts: 10 percent to United Silver Wings
  Club members
Conditions: club membership required

Aloha Airlines
800-367-5250
Discounts: low one-way rates; coupon book
  of six tickets is available
Conditions:
  Must be 65 years or older
  Must use tickets within one year

American Airlines
800-433-7300
Discounts:
  There are now three money-saving options
    with American Airlines
  Senior TrAAveler 10 percent discounts on all fares
  Senior TrAAveler coupon books
  Special AARP 10 percent discounts on flights
    booked 30 days in advance
  Other conditions apply
Conditions:
  Must be 62 years or older (AARP 50+)
  Must show proof of age when booking flight
  No tickets by mail
Bonus: one companion of any age may fly at the
  same fare

British Airways
(Same as British Caledonian)
British Caledonian
800-247-9297
Discounts:

Every departure city has its own senior rate

Privileged Traveller Program:

10 percent on any United Kingdom fares

10 percent on all travel packages

$10 fee for two years (six to eight weeks for application to be processed)

Your preferences are kept in their computer

Conditions:

Must be 60 years or older

Must book 14 days in advance

Must stay at least seven days and no longer than six months

$75 fee to change or cancel

Must travel Sunday through Wednesday going, Monday through Thursday returning

Bonus: a companion 50 years or older can travel at a reduced fare; members enjoy many privileges and amenities

Continental Airlines
800-525-0280
Discounts: 10 percent off any fare; Freedom

Passport — a year's worth of travel at a flat rate

Conditions:

Must be 62 years or older

Must show proof of age when booking or at departure; for tickets by mail, at departure

Bonus: one companion of any age can fly for the same fare

Delta

800-221-1212 or 800-843-9378

Discounts: a 10 percent Young-at-Heart Fare discount applies to most fares; Young-at-Heart coupon books — choose eight coupons or four coupons (Hawaii or Alaska require four coupons)

Conditions:

Must be 62 years or older

Coupons must be used within one year of first flight

May fly Tuesdays, Wednesdays, Thursdays, and Saturdays only

Reservations must be made no more than 6 1/2 days in advance of departure

Must stay over Saturday night

Book with coupons non-refundable after use of any portion

Upgrades don't apply for Frequent Flyers

Bonus: one companion of any age can receive
  a 10 percent discount

Finnair
800-950-5000
Discounts: economy fare discounts
Conditions:
  Must be 65 years or older
  Must book within three days of flight
  Fare is based on availability — no future
    reservations
  Return must be left open and booked within
    three days as well
  Ticket is good for one year from purchase
Bonus: spouses can travel at the same rate

KLM Royal Dutch Airlines
800-777-5553
Discounts: you must call for details
Conditions:
  Must be 60 years or older
  Must show proof of age
  Must book 14 days in advance
  Must return within six months
  Tickets are nontransferable and nonrefund-
    able
Bonus: your spouse can travel at the same
  rate

Lasca Airlines
800-225-2272
Discounts: lower rate each way, available year-round
Conditions:
   Must be 55 years or older
   Ticket good for one year

Lufthansa Airlines
800-645-3880
Discounts: check for specific discounts for economy-class only, excursion, and APEX fares
Conditions: must be 62 years or older
Bonus: companion fares are available

Midway Airlines
800-621-5700
Discounts: 10 percent on all fares, all destinations, year-round
Conditions: must be 62 years or older
Bonus: one companion can fly for the same fare

Mexicana
800-531-7921
Discounts: 10 percent on all flights
Conditions:
   Must be 62 years or older
   Not available from Los Angeles or San

Francisco to San Juan in July and August
Not available from San Juan to Mexico City
from April 15 to April 18 and December
15 to January 10
Bonus: one companion can fly for the same
fare

Northwest Airlines
(domestic) 800-225-2525
(international) 800-447-4747
Discounts: 10 percent on all flights, including
fourteen-day advance fares; World Horizons
Program (800-777-8585, ext. 555)
Conditions: must be 62 years or older
Bonus: one companion can fly for the same
fare; WorldPerks Senior savings for frequent
flyers is a way to fly free

Pan American Airways
800-221-1111
Discounts: 10 percent on all flights except
France and Russia; $45 flat rate between cit-
ies on shuttle flights
Conditions: must be 62 for most flights, 65
years or older for shuttle flights
Bonus: one companion can fly for the same
fare

Southwest Airlines
(See the White Pages for local listings in cities

served by this airline)

Discounts: promotional fares are seasonal, but they are excellent bargains when in effect

Conditions: must be 65 years or older; proof of age is required when booking

Transworld Airlines
(domestic) 800-221-2000
(international) 800-892-4141

Discounts: 10 percent on all domestic and international fares; TWA Take-Off Pass gives you 12 to 18 months of travel with a seven-day advance reservation

Conditions:

Must be 62 years or older

Travel is restricted to mid-week: Tuesday, Wednesday, and Thursday

Tel Aviv, Cairo, and Istanbul are excluded

Bonus: one companion can fly for the same fare

Swissair
800-221-4750

Discounts: senior fares are available

Conditions:

Must be 60 years or older

Must stay a minimum of seven days and a maximum of one year

Unavailable to Poland from June through September and between December 10 and 24

Unavailable to the U.S. between July 15 and September 30

United Airlines
800-241-6522
Discounts: 10 percent on all fares; Silver Wings Plus (800-628-2868) — $50 discount coupon with membership (a lifetime membership costs $50)
Conditions: must be 62 years or older
Bonus: one companion can fly for the same fare; club members enjoy discounts at Quality Inn, Ramada, Westin, and Hertz

USAir
800-428-4322
Discounts: 10 percent on all flights; discount coupon books are available
Conditions: must be 62 years or older with proof of age

Wardair
800-561-8686 (in Canada)
800-665-7783 (in Quebec)
Discounts: Global Horizons Club ($35 initiation, $20 annual fee) provides 10 percent off the lowest fares, Travel Savings Certificates, and other benefits; MasterCard, available for $45, comes with extra travel benefits

Conditions: must be 55 years or older
Bonus: one companion can join, regardless of
age

The airlines not mentioned do not have age-specific senior discount rates at this time. However, that does not mean that they don't have superior savings on fares published for the general public. Ask your travel agent to look at all airlines based on your particular travel needs.

Pets in Flight

If you can't bear to be apart from your pet even for a few days, make sure you have made plans for its health and safety.

- Find out the pet policies of the airline you are flying.
- Be sure to reserve a place — you want the cargo area to be pressurized, lighted, and temperature controlled.
- Contact your vet for a checkup and sedative if necessary.
- Let your pet become familiar with the flight-approved travel case (a tag will tell you if it has been cleared for air travel).
- Put something of yours, such as a sock, in the case with your pet for emotional security.

- Make sure your pet is welcome where you are going — some hotels permit pets, others don't, and relatives should not be forced to be hosts to your pet.

See the "Resources" chapter for more pet care information (pages 377-379).

Airline Hotlines

Air Canada	800-422-6232
Alaska Airline	800-426-0333
Alitalia Airlines	800-223-5730
Aloha Airlines	800-367-5250
American Airlines	800-433-7300
British Airways	800-247-9297
British Caledonian	800-247-9297
Continental Airlines	800-525-0280
Delta Airlines	800-221-1212 800-843-9378
Finnair	800-950-5000

KLM Royal Dutch	800-777-5553
Lasca Airlines	800-225-2272
Lufthansa Airlines	800-645-3880
Midway	800-621-5700
Mexicana	800-531-7921
Northwest Airlines	
Domestic	800-225-2525
International	800-447-4747
Pan American Airways	800-221-1111
Southwest Airlines	See local White Pages telephone directory
Swissair	800-221-4750
Transworld Airlines	
Domestic	800-221-2000
International	800-892-4141
United Airlines	800-241-6522
USAir	800-428-4322

Wardair
  In Canada   800-561-8686
  In Quebec   800-665-7783

Traveling by Car

Sometimes the most relaxing, and often the most economical, way to travel is by car. You can enjoy the flexibility of being able to come and go as you please, a plus if you are visiting with friends or relatives.

Car touring can be the perfect way to see the countryside, especially if you get off the freeways and explore the more scenic back roads. The Bureau of Land Management (see their address on page 299) has highlighted scenic roads through federal lands; a brochure printed by Farmers Insurance Group is available through your travel agent outlining these 35 designated back roads and byways. The U.S. Forest Service (page 299) has a similar program called National Forest Scenic Byways, which includes 3,000 miles of scenic byways in 27 states.

When traveling is to get you from one point to another, you want the best route available. Contact your motor club for individualized route planning. They will alert you to current construction problems or other road information that may affect your trip. Allow several weeks for your trip-planner kit to be completed and delivered to your home, particularly during peak travel seasons.

Motor clubs provide a security blanket of services to help you wherever you travel in the country. Most have a basic package of emergency road services and other benefits, but since it is a competitive market, you should shop for an auto club as carefully as you would any other service. The one or two services that make the most sense to you may not be available from every association. If you have an RV in addition to the family car, consider the Good Sam Emergency Road Service (see the Good Sam Club listing on page 302). Good Sam will cover your RV plus other cars, while many clubs will cover only your cars.

If you are traveling down the East Coast to Florida, you can take your car at least part of the way by train while you relax and enjoy the ride. Call Amtrak for information (800-USA-RAIL).

Car Rentals

With the association memberships and credit cards you hold, there is never a reason to pay full price for a car rental. Shop yourself, or have your travel agent check, to make sure you are getting the best deal available at the time you book your car. "Special" rates for AARP membership, as an example, are frequently higher than those you can obtain with some other affiliation or the rental companies' own promotional prices.

Renting a car involves a legal contract between you and the company covering the use of an expensive vehicle. Understanding the fine print is essential to prevent a financial disaster due to a liability you did not know you had. Even overlooking such items as gasoline charges can add significantly to your bill, an unpleasant surprise that can mar a trip and cut into your travel budget.

By doing some homework before you travel, you can make sure you are properly covered for your various liabilities and be knowlege-able enough to cut down on unnecessary add-on charges.

You also will want to find out important details, such as where the company desk is located (on or off airport property), which can affect your schedule when trying to catch a plane. For instance, some airports have conveniently located check-out desks, but you may discover that the rental return area is miles away from where you pick the car up. With remote lots, you may discover that you have to haul luggage, without assistance, in and out of buses and across parking lots. You need to know these details before deciding on a rental company; you may find that a higher rate will compensate for the inconvenience you must bear to get a lower price.

When you rent, make sure you have a clear understanding of:

- Insurance coverage, including liability, collision damage waiver, or loss damage waiver. Loss waiver, for example, protects you against theft and vandalism as well as damage caused by an accident. Some companies will want to transfer liability to your insurance policy. To cover potential losses, the company may block your credit card for a certain amount of money, which will reduce your spending power on that line of credit.

  Call your own insurance company to see what may be covered. Are you covered in any car you're driving? Are your belongings covered?

  Check with your credit card company to see if your card provides coverage so that you can decline the damage waiver and save $10 or more a day. American Express is one company that offers this service.

  A knowledgeable travel agent should know or be able to uncover the information that will let you arrange your coverage in the most beneficial way for your situation. You should know that, depending on the car company and your own insurance coverage, combined with certain credit card benefits, there simply are no stock answers. You must appraise your individual situation.

- Gas charges can be an unpleasant surprise. As a general rule, you will save money if you return the car with the same amount of gas as when they gave you the car. By-the-mile or fill-up charges are routinely more expensive than you would pay if buying the gas yourself. Beware of companies that start you off with half a tank but will not credit you if you bring the car back with a full tank. Expect legislation to bring some equity to this gray area of car rentals. In the meantime, ask about the policy beforehand.

- Geographic restrictions may prevent you from driving where you want to go. Depending on the demand for cars and other factors, you cannot count on driving outside the state. If you do, even out of ignorance, your insurance coverage may be void.

- Mileage charges can be computed for each mile driven, or packages may include specified miles or unlimited miles. If you choose according to your actual usage (by the mile for neighborhood driving, unlimited for extensive touring), you can have a fair rate. If you guess incorrectly, you could face stiff add-on charges.

- One-way or drop-off charges may apply if you wish to leave the car at an office other than the one from which you rented it. If there's any chance you may need to do so, find out about the policy ahead of time. In peak seasons, the penalty can be stiff; or, depending on the flow of cars within the system, you may be doing the company a favor by moving a unit to a higher-demand area.

- Time restrictions can penalize you for bringing the car back early or late. If you do not keep the car for the period of time specified in the contract, the company can revert to the more expensive day rate. If you're late, you may end up paying a premium price for those extra days.

- Check to see who is qualified to drive. If your spouse or other companion is not on the contract, he or she may not have the right to drive the car and may not have insurance coverage. If you are a 65+ driver, make sure the company you choose to rent from has no age maximum, or you may be denied a car when you arrive at the desk.

- Cars modified for handicapped individuals are available from most companies, but these normally must be reserved well in advance.

Chauffeured Tours

When traveling in foreign countries, some travelers have difficulty dealing with driving on the "wrong" side of the street, getting lost, or panicking in wild traffic. For these individuals, a chauffeured tour is the answer. Travelers sometimes arrange a day of guided private touring if they stop in a port city while on a cruise. Some simply enjoy the security of having an "insider" along when visiting areas that are new to them. In some countries, such as Greece, it is required that you have a driver and a guide.

Depending on the country and the company selected, these tours can range from a few hundred dollars to more than a thousand dollars a day, hotels and meals not included. You may enjoy the comfort of a Mercedes, Rolls-Royce, or other luxury car; the stretch limos generally are saved for airport pickups.

Typically you will be escorted by an English-speaking driver-guide who is fluent in the native language. You can see the sights or specify that you are looking for antiques, exclusive boutiques, or flower gardens. Best of all, you are not compelled to meet a prescribed schedule or visit the usual sights. You can get off the beaten track to experience a city or the countryside in a new way with someone who is in the know.

If this kind of individualized travel is appealing, it's best left to your travel agent to handle. The agent will contact one of the companies that specializes in this service, such as Abercrombie & Kent or AutoVenture, to arrange the details. Or, if you are already at your destination, the hotel concierge can arrange this service for you.

Clubs and Associations

In addition to the many organizations mentioned with the information on hotels and airlines, there are a number of clubs and associations that offer benefits ranging from travel discounts to lobbyists who defend 50+ issues in Washington, D.C. Most have small membership fees, but the costs are not listed here because they are likely to change.

American Association of Retired Persons
(AARP)
(202) 872-4700
Over the years, the AARP has become synonymous with the retired and semiretired consumer market and is a reputable source of information for the 50+ individual. AARP concerns itself with every aspect of life for its members, from travel to job opportunities, health care to insurance. It may be the best bargain available, considering the small membership fee and many outstanding benefits.

Encore Marketing International
4501 Forbes Boulevard, Suite 100
Lanham, MD 20706
800-638-8976

This Preferred Traveler Program gives members discounts at more than 2,400 hotels, motels, and resorts and at three major car rental agencies, plus guaranteed lowest airfares and bonus points toward free travel. The program is frequently offered through credit card companies, but it is available to anyone. Dues are relatively low, given the many discounts available.

Magic Years Club
PO Box 4709
Anaheim, CA 92803-4709
(714) 490-3250

Disney's world of magic opens to you as a member of this organization. Benefits range from discounts at Disneyland and Walt Disney World to meals, accommodations, and more. Many 50+ groups sell the memberships; you have the option of joining for life for a $25 fee.

Mature Outlook
6001 North Clark Street
Chicago, IL 60660
800-336-6330

This is the organization sponsored by the Sears Family of Companies. It offers a variety of services and discounts to members. There is an age minimum of 55.

Montgomery Ward Y.E.S. Discount Club
200 North Martingale Road
Schaumburg, IL 60173-2096
800-421-5396

Y.E.S. — Years of Extra Savings — was developed for the 55+ consumer (there is an age minimum of 55) to provide discounts on travel and merchandise. The low monthly dues ($2.90) can be charged to your Montgomery Ward account, VISA, or MasterCard. Well over a quarter of a million members enjoy the 40-percent discounts on more than 11,000 accommodations nationwide, and in addition you can receive 10-percent cash rebates when you return home.

Retired Officers Association
201 N. Washington Street
Alexandria, VA 22314-2529
(703) 549-2311

This organization provides a variety of travel services, tours, cruises, and more. Members also enjoy discounts on car rentals and special golf and tennis holidays. The Retired Officers Association also helps retired military officers with other issues, including entering the job market, health care insurance, and other life-style issues.

Traveler's Century Club
8033 Sunset Boulevard
Box 9
Los Angeles, CA 90046

This organization has an exclusive membership because of the requirement that members must have visited at least 100 countries, territories, or island groups. "Aspiring members" can join at a fraction of the usual annual membership fee and still receive the newsletter and join certain tours. This is an appealing group for those who are frequent, thoughtful travelers.

Last-Minute Travel Clubs

Moment's Notice
425 Madison Avenue
New York, NY 10017
(212) 486-0503

Spur of the Moment Cruises
10780 Jefferson Boulevard
Culver City, CA 90230
(213) 839-2418
800-343-1991
(213) 838-9329 (twenty-four-hour availability
   message)

Up 'n Go Travel
10 Mechanic Street
Worcester, MA 01608
(508) 792-5500

Worldwide Discount Travel Club
1674 Meridian Avenue
Miami Beach, FL 33139
(305) 534-2082

Associations: Activist Groups

Gray Panthers
1424 16th Street NW, Suite 602
Washington, D.C. 20036
(202) 387-3111
   This is an activist group that fights against ageism as it affects the workplace and other areas of life.

National Alliance of Senior Citizens
2525 Wilson Boulevard
Arlington, VA 22201
(703) 528-4380
   This is fundamentally a lobby group that takes up the causes of America's maturing population. They also produce a publication to inform members of issues and organizational activities.

National Council of Senior Citizens
925 Fifteenth Street NW
Washington, D.C. 20005
(202) 347-8800

This nonprofit organization provides a variety of services, including travel benefits, for members. There is a $12 membership fee.

Older Women's League
730 Eleventh Street NW, Suite 300
Washington, D.C. 20001
(202) 783-6686

This group is concerned with the issues facing older women in the nation. There's a bimonthly newsletter for members.

Services

The purpose of this book is to supply you with the information you need to fill your leisure time with travel, adventure, and education. Each section provides the resources that apply to that aspect of leisure or travel. This section is devoted to providing a number of miscellaneous resources you can tap into to make your leisure life-style even more rewarding, less expensive, and safer.

Insurance Protection

International SOS Assistance
1 Neshaminy Interplex
Trevose, PA 19047
(215) 244-1500 (in Pennsylvania)
800-523-8930

Wallach & Company
243 Church Street NW, Suite 100D
Vienna, VA 22180
800-237-6615

Travelers Insurance Companies
c/o Travel Pak
1 Tower Square
Hartford, CT 06115
800-243-3174

Air ambulance service — for members only:

Medical Air Services Association
800-643-9023 (for individual membership
    information)

Baggage protection:

International Airline Passengers Association
PO Box 60074
Dallas, TX 75266-0074
800-527-5888

Trip Cancellation Insurance

The insurance companies that offer temporary travel health insurance may offer trip cancellation insurance as well. Your travel agent, too, may offer a policy. Also check the following sources:

Access America
PO Box 11188
Richmond, VA 23230
800-654-6686

Travel Guard International
1145 Clark Street
Stevens Point, WI 54481
800-826-1300

Tele-Trip
3201 Farnam Street
Omaha, NE 68131
800-228-9999
Tele-Trip is in association with Mutual of Omaha.

Money to Go

American Express Gold Card
800-327-2177 (customer service)
American Express card members probably have the most financial flexibility when traveling of any of the travel and entertainment cardholders. (Some services have been reserved for Gold Card holders — call customer service for information.) Among the many services available are:

• American Express MoneyGram, to send (or

receive) $1,000 to $10,000 in an emergency.

- Global Assist, to get up to $5,000 for bail or hospital charges when you're out of the country, and for legal and medical referrals.
- Personal check-cashing privileges at hotels and American Express offices plus access to automatic teller machines (call 800-CASH-NOW).

American Express is like a security blanket when traveling domestically or worldwide. Its services are constantly expanding to better serve the traveling public and it has been known to handle travel emergencies for members even better than the American consulate.

Diners Club also offers a group of services for the traveler, including the International Service Center, which approves charges within seconds. You also can get instant cash, emergency assistance, and a variety of other services useful when traveling.

Other companies — both travel and entertainment card companies and credit card companies — are courting the traveler, too. Citicorp, as one example, is rapidly expanding to offer many of the same financial services for its customers as those offered by American Express. The best advice is to consult with your own travel and entertainment or credit card company's customer service department to find out what specific services may be offered for customers who travel.

UNICEF
333 East 38th Street
New York, NY 10016
(212) 686-5522
When you return from a trip and find that you have a pocket full of foreign change, UNICEF gladly will take it to fund its relief programs. Many travel organizations are helping in the collection of currency that otherwise would go unused.

Western Union
800-325-4176
Send cash, or have someone send it to you, using a VISA or MasterCard.

Pets

Pets Are Inn
27 North Fourth Street, Suite 500
Minneapolis, MN 55401
(612) 339-6255
800-248-PETS
This service provides a guilt-reducing alternative to boarding the family pet. Caretakers offer a foster home for small animals while you travel. Your pet gets lots of attention after

it is matched by computer with a compatible caretaker in your area. Every caretaker is a pet lover and must provide references. Many caretakers who apply travel themselves, so they understand the anguish of leaving a pet in a kennel or unattended with a "sitter" who rushes in to feed the pet every day.

A large percentage of the caretakers are retirees who enjoy the company of a pet but not the commitment of full-time pet ownership. Pets are picked up and delivered. If you travel frequently, the service will try to get your pet boarded with the same caretaker on subsequent trips. Clients get to see a picture of where their pet will stay, but the caretakers remain unknown to the owners (to prevent the caretakers from having to reassure nervous owners by phone that their pets are fine). This is a loving, practical solution for pet owners. Franchises are popping up across the country, so there may be a service in your community as well.

DO-IT
Bud Brownhill
2147 Avon Circle
Anaheim, CA 92804

DO-IT, Dog Owners for International Travel, was formed when Bud Brownhill's prized pet was misdirected on a flight and deafened by roaring jets. If you have concerns or need information about pets in flight, this is an organization that will give you support with the airline industry.

Telephones

AT & T
800-874-4000, ext. 374
Those annoying surcharges hotels put on your overseas long distance phone calls can add up to give you an unpleasant surprise when you check out. Through its USA Direct plan, AT & T is giving you a way to lower or eliminate surcharges.

Travel Complaints

Check out any travel organization ahead of time or register a complaint after the fact with the people who can make a difference.

American Society of Travel Agents
Consumer Affairs Department
PO Box 23992
Alexandria, VA 20026-3992
(703) 739-2782
ASTA keeps track of complaints against tour operators and travel agencies. It can act as an informal liaison between you and a

company to settle problems.

Amtrak
(202) 906-2121 (customer relations department)
Contact this office if you have any complaints about train service on Amtrak.

Better Business Bureau
(Your area office is listed in the White Pages)
The Better Business Bureau records complaints and resolutions regarding businesses, including operators and agencies, in your area.

U.S. Department of Transportation
Consumer Affairs Office
(202) 366-2220
These are the people to contact about problems with the airlines.

Federal Aviation Administration (FAA)
Consumer Hotline
800-322-7873
This agency is responsible for carry-on baggage problems and airport security.

Federal Aviation Administration
Safety Hotline
800-255-1111
This division fields reports on safety problems on planes.

Travel Lobbyists

International Airline Passengers Association (IAPA)
Box 660074
Dallas, TX 75266-0074
800-527-5888

Offering complete travel services to its members, the IAPA also provides discounts, a Bag Guard luggage tracking system, insurance, representation in Washington, D.C., and more. This is an organization that serves the frequent traveler well.

Travel Opportunities Through Employment

If your heart is in travel, one of the best ways to fulfill your dreams is to get a job in the industry.

International Executive Corps
Box 10005
Stamford, CT 06904-2005
(203) 967-6000

This organization sends retired executives and technical support personnel to various countries around the world to help develop local industries and economies. Exercise your talents and travel, too, by joining this program.

American Hotel and Motel Association
1201 New York Avenue NW
Washington, D.C. 20005

Send a self-addressed, stamped envelope to this trade association to receive information about the job opportunities for mature employees in this industry. There are part-time and flex-time opportunities to fit most schedules. Best of all, as an insider you often will be extended professional courtesies and discounts when you travel.

Weather

Two weather services give you reliable information to help you pack for short trips. As 900 numbers, you will be charged a small fee on your telephone bill for this information.

1-900-WEATHER

Dial this service and add the three digits of the area code where you plan to travel or the first three letters of the international city where you plan to go. This service is a joint effort between American Express and Accu-Weather.

1-900-370-USAT

This is the weather service provided by the newspaper *USA Today*.

Health and Safety

There is a new medical specialty called *emporiatrics* (from the Greek word *empros*, or traveler). Travel-related illnesses can be an annoying inconvenience or a major problem if you are far from home. Emporiatrics addresses the specific ailments that trouble travelers. To maintain health and comfort, make some practical pretrip preparations, follow some sensible on-the-road guidelines, and watch for possible post-trip problems.

Check With Your Doctor

See your physician. Emporiatrics specialist Kenneth R. Dardick, M.D., F.A.C.P., believes that with a team effort between the physician and patient, 50 to 75 percent of travel ills can be prevented. Part of maintaining health during and after a trip is being aware of the potential problems of the areas you plan to visit.

Although you are not required to have a long list of immunizations, you may wish to take precautions anyway. Diseases that may be under control in the U.S. still pose a threat elsewhere. Your physician has access to publications issued by the Center for Disease

Control and a quarterly publication called *Travel Medicine International.*

However, many general practitioners are not, and cannot be, up-to-date with the many conditions worldwide that may affect your health. A computerized Immunization Alert data base developed by Dr. Dardick gives up-to-the-minute information you need to protect yourself when traveling internationally. Dr. Dardick points out that the guidelines for immunization traveling out of and back into the U.S. are easy to understand. However, should you be traveling between several foreign countries during your trip, you may encounter obstacles if there are recent changes that you, your doctor, and your travel agent may not have known about.

Many physicians and health organizations subscribe to this computer data base, which is updated weekly using World Health Organization and Center for Disease Control information. However, if you are unable to locate someone who uses the service, you can contact Dr. Dardick directly. If you supply him with your itinerary, including the order in which various countries will be visited, you can receive a printout that you can take to your own doctor. The fee is nominal. See the "Health Resources" section (pages 398-401) for details.

For a full set of immunizations, allow several weeks. Various shots need a spaced schedule. You can conveniently carry your immunization records in an International Certificate of Vaccinations folder, available at the health department or from your travel agent.

When you see your doctor, secure the following, whether traveling domestically or internationally:

- Prescriptions for all medications you will need. Take an ample supply in case you extend your stay.
- A list of the generic names of the medications you take, since name brands may be different where you travel.
- A brief summary of your medical history, including pertinent information about any conditions for which you currently are being treated.
- A copy of a recent electrocardiogram, even if you have no history of heart problems (it's a convenient baseline comparison should you have problems away from home).
- To speed you through a security check, a letter from your doctor explaining any implant, artificial joint, or other unseen medical appliance that may trigger the metal detector at the airport.

- A list of your doctor's colleagues in the area you plan to travel.

See Your Dentist

- Have all dental problems repaired well in advance of when you fly (this ensures that the change in cabin pressure will not cause unnecessary pain in new dental work).
- Secure a second or temporary appliance should your bridgework get broken during travel.
- If possible, obtain a list of your dentist's colleagues in the area you plan to visit.

See Your Eye Doctor

- Obtain a spare pair of glasses or contacts and a copy of your prescription.
- Buy prescription or clip-on sunglasses.

Pack Your Medical Travel Kit

- Pack your prescriptions in clearly marked plastic prescription bottles. There's no need to raise the suspicions of nervous customs officials by having your various pills unidentified in plain bottles. Take more than enough, in case there are delays. Keep your prescriptions with you, in case your luggage is delayed or lost. Some smart travelers split their medications, in case their carry-on bag or purse is lost or stolen.

- Pack a first-aid kit: antiseptic, gauze, cotton balls, pain ointment, adhesive bandages, adhesive tape, and foot or toe pads.
- Pack over-the-counter drugs that may not be readily available during your travels: a pain reliever, antacids, digestive tract medication, a laxative, decongestant or nose spray, a motion sickness preventive, such as the convenient Transderm-Scop patch, which is worn behind the ear.
- Pack convenient home-remedy instruments: thermometer (in a break-proof carrier), scissors, and tweezers.
- Sunscreen and insect repellent.
- For muscle fatigue, strain, or injury, you might want to pack support socks or hose and elastic bandages.

Pack an In-Flight Comfort Kit

- Saline nose spray (non medicated) for dry air in planes.
- Skin cream, to combat dryness.
- Inflatable neck pillow.
- An emergency "nibble" pack, in case of delays. It might include granola bars or dried fruit.

Insurance Protection

You also will want to contact your insurance carrier to see how and what they will cover if you are sick or injured while traveling. Even if you are covered, you may have to pay for any medical costs before coming home and the insurance company will reimburse you. You may want to take proper insurance claim forms with you for the doctor or hospital to fill out, to make sure your claim is not delayed for lack of proper documentation. Failing that, be sure that all of your paperwork outlines clearly what you were treated for and what you paid. Medicare does not pay for any services out of the country; Medicare supplemental insurance may cover some services.

Fill any insurance gaps with temporary traveler's insurance. These policies may cover a variety of potential losses in addition to the medical coverage, including lost luggage and trip cancellation. Typically these policies are offered through your own insurance company or your travel agent. (See "Health Resources" directory starting on page 398).

One type of travel protection you should have is in the form of proper medical ID. For a modest price, most pharmacies offer simple ID bracelets and necklaces with information about allergies or other medical problems. If you can't find them, contact Health Enterprises (800-MEDIC-ID).

For more comprehensive coverage, the Medic Alert foundation will register your medical information in an emergency data bank for retrieval from any phone by a health professional. The familiar Medic Alert bracelets are part of the service provided for a nominal registration fee. Contact Medic Alert at 800-344-3226.

You also may want to leave on your trip secure in the knowledge that you have help at hand should you need it. American Express card members can access the Global Assist Hotline to find physicians in cities around the world. The International Association for Medical Assistance to Travelers (IAMAT) is a well-known organization that supplies the names of English-speaking doctors around the world. A members-only service also is provided by WorldCare. Be sure you have complete information and membership in one of these services before you leave. See "Health Resources" (page 398) for contact numbers.

Another service that is gaining in popularity is membership in one of the air ambulance associations. Should you become ill away from home, they will fly you by air ambulance, with medical personnel, to your home hospital or to the best medical facility close to you. If you're stranded for more than a week, you can have a family member or companion flown to be with you. Should you be brought home, the service will arrange to have your car or RV driven to your home. There are a variety of other services available, depending on the organization.

The advantage of membership in an air ambulance group is savings. On your own, you would have to pay, in cash, a fee of up to $10,000 or more before the plane took off (Medicare now reimburses for certain approved air ambulance services from an approved Medicare provider; check for specifics, since these rules change). This industry is currently unregulated, however, so it is wise to join an established association with a good reputation. The fees vary considerably, too. If you can join such a group as an optional benefit through another association to which you belong, your annual fees are likely to be significantly lower.

One of the pioneers in the industry is the Medical Air Services Association (800-643-9023) which will provide service to members traveling outside the continental United States, including Hawaii, Alaska, Canada,

Mexico, or the Caribbean. Although any traveler can join, it is gaining a significant reputation among RV owners who want the security of getting themselves, and their vehicles, home if there is a medical emergency.

Call Ahead for Special Services

If you are going to need special medical attention — or just some personal pampering — call ahead or have your travel agent contact the airline, cruise ship, or hotels. The airline can transport you from terminal to terminal on a people-mover vehicle or via wheelchair, even if you are not handicapped but just cannot rush through crowds. If your condition warrants, you can arrange for in-flight oxygen, but be prepared to answer some probing medical questions (they don't want you to have problems they cannot adequately handle). They also will meet your special food needs en route with at least 24-hours' notice, sometimes longer.

Cruise ships and hotels will be happy to accommodate your special needs, from refrigeration of medication to special menus. However, they can serve you much better if they know ahead of time what your exact needs may be.

If visiting for a period of time in one city,

call ahead or have your doctor phone to make sure you can have routine blood tests (if needed to balance medication) or other clinical services. When the way has been prepared ahead of time, you won't waste precious vacation hours trying to secure attention for simple medical needs.

On the Road

With the resources outlined in this book that encourage you to exercise and stick to your healthy eating plan, you have the best opportunity to keep healthy while traveling. If you completely abandon your normally healthy eating habits and exercise routine while traveling, you may find yourself more susceptible to illness and other physical problems.

According to experts, there are two main travel-related health care problems: environment-related, and organism-induced problems. An environment-related problem would include motion sickness or jet lag. An organism-related problem might be the ever-present *turista*.

Jet lag is easily handled with some no-nonsense guidelines. Keep alcohol and caffeine consumption down, eat light, and drink plenty of water. Get on the local schedule as soon as you can, but allow your body to "reset" comfortably by getting plenty of rest and not overtaxing yourself when you first arrive. Experienced travelers have adopted this motto from Anthony N. Nicholson, M.D., of the Royal Air Force: fly east, fly early; fly west, fly late. This gives you the best chance to get "on schedule" with local time, both coming and going.

Remember, to avoid stomach upsets, do not drink tap water. You may forget not to have drinks with ice cubes and you may not know that well-meaning hotel personnel have refilled your water bottles with tap water. Also, while you may feel safe in the U.S., some people react simply from *any* change in the water. So for the most part, drink carbonated water and juices.

Avoid fresh raw vegetables, which may have been washed in tap water. Peel your own fruit. Be wary of dishes with dairy products or foods served at room temperature (food should be served well cooked and hot, or cold right from the refrigerator).

Some travelers take papaya tablets from the health food store to aid digestion or bottles of liquid oxygen to drop into reportedly "safe" water. Both have been reported to give the body aid in handling unfriendly organisms, preventing the annoyance of *turista*. However, this is considered not conventional medical treatment but rather a holistic health alternative.

If you suffer a serious injury or a critical illness, what should you do?

- Immediately contact your tour guide (if you are on a guided trip), hotel manager, or cruise director.
- Contact your medical reference service, provided through the membership you secured before departure (American Express Global Assist is one example).
- If all else fails, call the American consulate. Call the embassy only if there is no other alternative. They have someone to answer emergency calls 24 hours a day.

When You Get Home

Take it easy. Resume your normal routine, but be gentle on yourself. Travel is stressful, even when everything goes perfectly and you have a wonderful time. If you should develop symptoms within weeks, even months, after a trip, remember to tell your doctor where you traveled and when. Note if you had any symptoms while traveling or suffered from any bites (mosquitos or ticks). Such information may speed up the diagnosis and your treatment.

Travel Health Information

If you travel frequently, you may want to subscribe to an informative publication called the *Healthy Traveler*. You may have seen a complimentary copy at larger hotels, but this magazine is packed with the kind of information healthy travelers want. Subscribers get many bonus items, such as monthly premiums and coupons, a medical ID card, and other related items. (See "Health Resources," page 398.)

Travel Safety

There's no need to spoil a potentially wonderful trip with paranoia about the possible dangers you may encounter. Nonetheless, a bit of caution can go a long way toward keeping you and your belongings safe.

- Guard your passport carefully. American passports are worth thousands of dollars on the black market. For an immediate temporary replacement, contact the American embassy or consulate right away if yours is lost or stolen.
- Protect your valuables. Many savvy travelers don't risk wearing prized jewelry. Simple jewelry is less likely to draw un-

wanted attention to you. If you must take jewelry, use hotel or ship lockboxes or the new in-room safes. They are your only practical protection.

- Consider the baggage insurance offered by some credit card companies. Also, look into baggage tracing systems, such as the one offered to members by International Airline Passengers (800-527-5888).
- Don't flash cash. This should be obvious, but in the excitement of negotiating in a bazaar or after partying in a local restaurant, some people forget to handle money discreetly.

Credit cards are convenient means of handling transactions, but watch your statement carefully for overcharges and exchange rates when you get home. Use a credit card when you ask a shop to ship items home, so you will have recourse if the merchandise does not arrive.

Travelers checks are safe, too, but they are convenient only in lower denominations.

- Check with your travel agent or the hotel itself to make sure you will be protected by smoke alarms. Some hotels do not have them. Consider buying a portable unit to take with you.
- Take the time to read the emergency in-

formation when you check in. Count the doors to the exits in case smoke clouds your vision in an emergency.

- Remember, many hotel room doors automatically lock when they close. Take your key in an emergency, just in case you'd be safer staying in your room.
- Half of all hotel fires start with a guest smoking in bed. A weary traveler is more likely to drop off to sleep while smoking. Use common sense: *never smoke in bed.*
- When flying, no matter how frequently you have boarded a plane, always pay attention to the flight attendants during their safety instructions and count the seats to the nearest exit.

Cooperate with cruise directors when safety drills are given. These instructions are given to save *your* life!

- Never agree to carry a parcel or suitcase for a stranger or casual acquaintance unless you know with certainty what is inside.
- Watch your luggage at the terminal to make sure nothing is taken, and also to make sure that someone doesn't slip something that doesn't belong to you among your possessions.
- With increased security concerns, be prepared for bags to be searched and delays to occur.

- For your passport, cash, and credit cards, you may want to invest in a money belt or a pouch-type wallet that is worn inside the clothes, suspended by a string that goes around your neck. These are especially useful in foreign cities where purse snatching is a problem.

Health Resources

Medical Help While Traveling

Global Assist
(202) 783-7474 (collect, from overseas)
800-554-AMEX (domestic calls)
This service is for American Express card members only. For information about the program, call the number on your card.

International Association for Medical
Assistance to Travelers (IAMAT)
417 Center Street
Lewiston, NY 14092
(716) 754-4883

WorldCare
(202) 293-0335 (for information)

U.S. State Department
Citizens Emergency Center
(202) 647-5225

Medical Information Services

Medical ID:

Health Enterprises
15 Spruce Street
Attleboro, MA 02760
(508) 695-0727
800-MEDIC-ID
   Your medical information is engraved on
jewelry in case of emergency. Order forms are
available at most pharmacies.

ID and computer data base:

Medic Alert
PO Box 1009
Turlock, CA 95381
(209) 668-3333 (in California)
800-344-3226

Health Publications

Healthy Traveler
410 East Water Street
Charlottesville, VA 22901
(804) 296-5676
   The *Healthy Traveler* is a magazine.

The Johns Hopkins Medical Letter
Health After 50
PO Box 420179
Palm Coast, FL 32142
   This moderately priced newsletter addresses the health issues of those over 50.

Upjohn: Jet Lag Booklet
Box B307
Coventry, CT O6238
   You can get this booklet free from Upjohn at the above address.

Jet Lag Diet
Argonne National Laboratories
Department BH
9700 South Cass
Argonne, IL 60439
   Get the *Jet Lag Diet* free by sending a self-addressed, stamped envelope to the above address.

Immunizations

Immunization Alert
Kenneth Dardick, M.D.
PO Box 406
Storrs, CT 06268
(203) 487-0422
Refer to the "Insurance Protection" section
(pages 388-391) for insurance information.

Nonsmoking Accommodations

For a nonsmoker, having to stay in a stuffy room with the lingering odor of stale smoke is one of the least-pleasant aspects of a trip. However, since public opinion has swung substantially to the side of nonsmokers, hotels and motels are responding with nonsmoking rooms.

Some hotels have designated rooms for non-smokers, and others have designated floors; many (not listed here) restrict smoking in certain public areas. At the Sheraton Denver Tech Center, the maids are even forbidden to smoke while cleaning on the nonsmoking floors! Some, such as the Cliff Spa, Canyon Ranch, the Non-Smokers Inn, and the Sterling Hotel are smoke-free throughout.

Every month, more hotels are succumbing to consumer pressure to provide this amenity. Be sure to ask if your favorite hotel is not on this list of industry leaders. In fact, the more often you ask, the more likely there will be additional nonsmoking rooms available across the country.

Canyon Ranch
Tucson, AZ
800-742-9000

Colony Parke Hotel
Dallas, TX
(214) 750-6060

Compri Hotels
800-4-COMPRI

Days Inn
800-241-5050

Four Seasons
(Some locations)
800-332-3442

Hyatt Regency Scottsdale
Scottsdale, AZ
800-228-9000

Non-Smokers Inn
Dallas, TX
(214) 631-6633

Quality International
800-221-2222

Red Lion Inns
800-547-8010

Sheraton Denver Tech Center
Denver, CO
800-325-3535

Snowbird Cliff Spa
Snowbird, UT
(801) 742-2222, ext. 5900

Sonesta Hotels
(Boston and Portland locations)
800-SONESTA

Sterling Hotel
Sacramento, CA
800-365-7660

Westin Hotels
(Dallas and Fort Lauderdale locations)
800-228-3000

Vagabond Inns
800-522-1555

Smoking is also restricted on Mayflower tours, Domenico tours, and California Parlour car tours, and on Outward Bound adventures.

The Handicapped Traveler

Although virtually all new public buildings are by law including handicapped-access facilities, many older buildings are not as convenient. With advance notice, hotels, in an effort to make your stay as enjoyable as possible, will do whatever they can for you. Some hotels are actively seeking your business by providing the facilities that are ideal for you.

Information services are available to help you plan your trip if you have a disability.

American Council of the Blind
1155 15th NW, Suite 720
Washington, D.C. 20005
(202) 467-5081
This organization provides a list of publications, including tour information, for disabled travelers.

American Hotel and Motel Association
1201 New York Avenue NW
Washington, D.C. 20005
(202) 289-3100
In its *Tips for Travelers* pamphlet, this association provides information about travel in general and specific services for the disabled.

Send $1 plus a long, self-addressed, stamped envelope with two first-class stamps.

Conference of National Park Concessionaires
Mammoth Cave, KY 42259
(502) 773-2191
Along with general information about accommodations and services in the national park system, there is information about facilities for the disabled.

Consumer Information Center
Box 100
Pueblo, CO 81002
Write for the free booklet *Access Travel* (number 563W), which outlines airport access in more than five hundred airports in sixty-two countries.

National Library Service for the Blind
  and Physically Disabled
Library of Congress
Reference Section
Washington, D.C. 20542
Write for the free booklet *Information for Handicapped Travelers*. It contains information about specialized books, services, and even travel agents for the disabled.

Travel Information Service
Moss Rehabilitation Hospital
Twelfth Street and Tabor Road
Philadelphia, PA 19141
(215) 456-9603

This is an educational service of the hospital. The department serves as a learning house of specialized information for travelers. Material, including personal reports, are filed by destination. There is a postage and handling charge of $5 (3 destinations).

U.S. Department of the Interior
Information Office
Eighteenth and C Streets
Washington, D.C. 20240

If you are blind or permanently disabled, you qualify for a Golden Access Passport for free entrance to parks operated by the federal government and 50-percent discounts on such items as camping fees. Passports are issued in person only to those who provide proof of their disability. Passports are available through most national parks and regional park offices. The Information Office of the Department of the Interior can provide a listing of offices in your area.

Telephone Numbers for
Hearing Impaired

Transportation

American Airlines
800-582-1573

Continental Airlines
800-343-9195

Delta Airlines
800-831-4488

Northwest Airlines
800-328-2298

Pan American Airways
800-722-3323

Southwest Airlines
800-533-1305

Trans World Airlines
800-421-8480
800-252-0622 (in California)

United Airlines
800-323-0170
800-942-8819 (in Illinois)

U.S. Air
800-334-5874
800-242-1713 (in Pennsylvania)

Amtrak
800-523-6590 (TDD/TTY toll-free reservation line)
800-562-6960 (in Pennsylvania)

Greyhound Bus Lines
800-345-3109

Accommodations

Four Seasons
2800 North Pennsylvania
Washington, D.C. 20007
800-332-3442
   This hotel provides services for the hearing
impaired.

Hampton Inns
800-451-HTDD (TDD toll-free reservation
line)
   This hotel chain has visual-alert systems for
the hearing impaired.

Holiday Inns
800-238-5544 (TDD toll-free reservation
line)

Omni Ambassador East
1301 North State Parkway
Chicago, IL 60610
800-THE-OMNI
   Rarely seen in hotels, the Omni has installed smoke detectors designed for the safety of the hearing impaired.

Super 8 Motels
800-533-6634 (TDD toll-free reservation line)

Travel Information

Michigan Travel Bureau
PO Box 30226
Lansing, MI 48909
800-722-8191 (TDD toll-free reservation line, in Michigan only)

Minnesota Office of Tourism
375 Jackson Street
250 Skyway Level
St. Paul, MN 55101
(TDD toll-free relay service in Minnesota for the hearing impaired)
800-657-3529

Handicapped Access

The hotels listed here have designated handicapped-access rooms. Some have just a few rooms available, so it is important to secure your reservation as early as possible. Others, such as the Westin Cypress Creek, have as many as 30 rooms available. Surprisingly, even the historic Dunlap House, a quaint bed-and-breakfast, can accommodate handicapped guests, thanks to a renovation that preserved the charm while adding contemporary amenities.

Arrowwood
A Doral Property
Anderson Hill Road
Rye Brook, NY 10573
(914) 939-5500

Dunlap House
635 Green Street
Gainesville, GA 30501
(404) 536-0200

Four Seasons
1 Logan Square
Philadelphia, PA 19103
800-332-3442

Four Seasons
2800 North Pennsylvania Avenue
Washington, D.C. 20007
800-332-3442

Loew's Ventana Canyon Resort
7000 North Resort Drive
Tucson, AZ 85715
(602) 299-2020
800-223-0888

Omni Ambassador East
1301 North State Parkway
Chicago, IL 60610
800-THE-OMNI

Opryland USA
2802 Opryland Drive
Nashville, TN 37214
(615) 889-6600
(615) 889-6611

Red Lion Inns
800-547-8010

Sheraton Monterey
350 Calle Principal
Monterey, CA 93940
800-325-3535

Super 8 Motels
800-843-1991

Vagabond Inns
800-522-1555

Three travel companies also have special access/accommodations for the handicapped:

Amtrak
800-USA-RAIL
Amtrak has special facilities available as well as a booklet called *Access Amtrak.*

Greyhound Bus Lines
901 North Main
Dallas, TX 75202
(214) 744-6509
Greyhound provides a booklet called *Helping Hand Services for the Handicapped.*

Admiral Cruises
1050 Caribbean Way
PO Box 010882
Miami, FL 33132
(305) 374-1611
800-327-0271
Admiral Cruises feature a fully accessible cabin for cruises.

For Information About Handicapped Access by State

Florida Department of Commerce
  Visitors Inquiry
126 Van Buren Street
Tallahassee, FL 32301-2000
(904) 487-1462

Minnesota Office of Tourism
375 Jackson Street
250 Skyway Level
St. Paul, MN 55101
(612) 296-5029 (in St. Paul and Minneapolis)
800-652-9747 (in Minnesota)
The Minnesota Office of Tourism, in cooperation with the Minnesota Council on Disability, has created an impressive 12-page access guide. There is information about camping, attractions, sports programs, transportation, and more. The guide also lists many organizations and a variety of useful publications if you plan a trip to the state.

North Carolina Division of Travel
  and Tourism
430 North Salisbury Street
Raleigh, NC 27611
(919) 733-4171
800-VISIT-NC

Information about accessibility is incorporated into their promotional magazine.

Virginia Department of Tourism
202 North Ninth Street, Suite 500
Richmond, VA 23219
(804) 786-4484

The Virginia Travel Guide for the Disabled is published by the Opening Door as the first in an ambitious series that will provide comprehensive information about accommodations, restaurants, and public buildings. It is detailed, with specific information about widths of doors, whether bathroom doors open in or out, and much other access-smart information. The book is free to the disabled but costs others $5.

Handicapped RV Travel

A long list of manufacturers that modify vehicles for disabled RVers is available from RVIA. With handicapped facilities still somewhat limited in mainstream hotels and resorts, the convenience of having a custom-designed bring-your-own accommodations can be appealing to the handicapped traveler. Be sure to order the brochure previously mentioned on camping in the national parks (see page 298). You can discover the accessible campgrounds in

Prevention
33 East Minor Street
Emmaus, PA 18098

A monthly magazine, *Prevention* is filled with nutritional and medical information. Although it is family-oriented, many 50+ readers are among the subscribers. The emphasis is on a balanced, natural life-style. This is the magazine that sponsors a walking club with members throughout the country (See "Walking and Cycling," pages 69-76).

Rockport Walking Program, by Dr. James M. Rippe and Ann Ward, Ph.D., with Karla Dougherty

Spa Finder
784 Broadway
New York, NY 10003-4856
(212) 475-1000

This beautiful magazine is actually a catalog of the most glorious spas around. Complete information is detailed to help you choose the spa for you. This is the publishing extension of the Spa Finders travel organization. They know what they are talking about!

Specialty Travel
305 San Anselmo Avenue, Suite 217
San Anselmo, CA 94960
(415) 459-4900

If your taste runs to the exotic, or at least the adventurous, take note of this magazine, which is packed with intriguing travel options. This publication is targeted primarily at the travel industry, so you can count on plenty of insider information.

Today's Seniors
1091 Brevik Place
Mississauga, Ontario, Canada L4W 3R7
(416) 238-0555

This lively newspaper is distributed free to the 50+ crowd in Toronto and several other metropolitan areas. It also is available for home delivery. Readers can enjoy the benefits of Club 50 Plus as well when they join for a $17.95 fee.

Index

430

440

The employees of THORNDIKE PRESS hope you have enjoyed this Large Print book. All our Large Print titles are designed for easy reading, and all our books are made to last. Other Thorndike Large Print books are available at your library, through selected bookstores, or directly from us. For more information about current and upcoming titles, please call or mail your name and address to: